OOR · PLAN ·

1/16" = 1'.0"
ELEVATION

·SCALE· FOR·PLAN & ELEVATION·

·SECTION·

MEAS & DRAWN· KENNETH CLARK·

ING·ISSUE·OF·
GRAPH·SERIES·
CONTAIN· MEASURED
DRAWINGS·OF·THE·INTERIOR
OF·THE·BRICE·HOUSE·

E V A T I O N ·

E · H O U S E ·

· M A R Y L A N D ·

EARLY AMERICAN
COMMUNITY STRUCTURES

EARLY AMERICAN COMMUNITY STRUCTURES

From material originally published as
The White Pine Series of Architectural Monographs
edited by
Russell F. Whitehead and Frank Chouteau Brown

Lisa C. Mullins, Editor

Roy Underhill, Consultant

A Publication of
THE NATIONAL HISTORICAL SOCIETY

Library of Congress Cataloging-in-Publication Data

The Evolution of colonial architecture.
  (Architectural treasures of Early America; 9)
    1. Architecture, Domestic — New England.   2. Architecture, Colonial — New England.   3. Decoration and ornament, Architectural — New England.   4. Building, Brick — New England.   I. Mullins, Lisa C.   II. Underhill, Roy.   III. National Historical Society.   IV. Series: Architectural treasures of Early America (Harrisburg, Pa.); 9.
NA7210.E96   1988   720′.974   87-14206
ISBN 0-918678-28-5

The original photographs reproduced in this publication are from the collection of drawings and photographs in "The White Pine Monograph Series, Collected and Edited by Russell F. Whitehead, The George P. Lindsay Collection." The collection, part of the research and reference collections of The American Institute of Architects, Washington, D.C., was acquired by the Institute in 1955 from the Whitehead estate, through the cooperation of Mrs. Russell F. Whitehead, and the generosity of the Weyerhauser Timber Company, which purchased the collection for presentation to the Institute. The research and reference collections of the Institute are available for public use. A written request for such use is required so that space may be reserved and assistance made available.

CONTENTS

THE UNDERTAKER

"We hear from Stafford County in Viginia, that the new Church at Aquia, one of the Best Buildings in that Colony (and the old Wooden one near it) were burnt down on the 17th Instant, by the Carelessness of some of the Carpenters leaving Fire too near the Shavings, at Night, when they left off Work. This fine Building was within two or three Days Work of being completely finished and delivered up by the Undertaker, and this Accident, it is said, has ruin'd him and his Securities."

from *The Pennsylvania Gazette*, March 25, 1755.

His name was Mourning Richards, and it seemed that he was out of luck. He was the undertaker, the prime contractor, for the Aquia church; subcontracting the work to the carpenters and bricklayers. Legally, a building under construction remained the undertaker's property until it was completed and accepted by the church. The undertaker was typically paid in thirds: one-third to begin, one-third when the walls were up, one-third upon completion. Richards had already been paid by the vestry, so now he was going to have to rebuild the church out of his own pocket. He looked like a ruined man, but, where public money is concerned, nothing is that simple.

To pay the undertaker for a public building, money had to come from the pockets of the people, either by consensus or coercion. In colonies where the Anglican church was established, everyone, even dissenters, had to pay taxes for the parish. According to Carl Lounsbury, an architectural historian specializing in early American public buildings, this factor affected the survival of colonial structures. Most of the churches that survive in South Carolina are solid brick Anglican parish churches. But, if you look at the composition of the society in South Carolina, the Anglicans were just one among many denominations. Because they were the established church, they could take tax money and build churches that would last. Other denominations, running on faith alone, could only afford frame buildings that did not endure.

Secular public buildings could also generate dissention. In towns in New England, there was an obvious central space for markets, meetings, and court houses. In the rural south, however, there was no need for a central market, and hence, no towns. There was no natural spot to put a county court house. It took a lot of arguing before the first gavel could fall in the new building.

Once they decided where to put it, the church vestry or the county building committee determined the size of the building, based on the size of their purse. Would it be brick or frame, one or two stories? The design often followed neighboring examples, generally striving to be a little grander than that of the next county, or the next parish over.

Court houses had to go for style on the cheap. There was a limit to the taxes that the people were willing to pay. Court houses ran from one-half to two-thirds the cost of a church of equal size. Often, court house finish work would literally cut corners. In the

Edenton, North Carolina, court house, one of the few colonial court houses to survive, the wainscotted justice's bench is curved to match the apse wall. It looks impressive, but if you step past the bar to look at it more closely, you will see that it is actually faceted, the individual panels are flat, not curved. The effect is grand, the execution cheap.

Penny pinching and fires were not the only problems the undertaker of a public building had to face. Distinct from modern practice, where you get the blueprints and stick to them, colonial plans changed as the work progressed. The building committee, along with the undertaker, wrote up specifications, but specifications such as "neat and plain" are wide open to interpretation. When the committee started putting in windows and tearing down walls as fast as they went up, they quickly fouled up any overall architectural theme. Design by committee was not just a joke in early American building.

Perhaps it was simpler in the early days when people met in taverns to solve their problems. In the seventeenth century, privately owned taverns functioned as public buildings. When churches and court houses were first built, they looked like ordinary houses with ordinary rooms. But from the seventeenth century to the end of the eighteenth century, public buildings changed. They went from multipurpose, generalized structures, to those that exhibit what's going on inside by the appearance of the outside. The interior became increasingly specialized as well. When the law develops specific regulations and procedures—when you get treasurers, inspectors, controllers, and sheriffs—then each must have a specialized place. You can't have a bureaucracy without a proper place to put it.

The court house in Williamsburg, Virginia, was a typical project. For years the court met in a theater, and before that, perhaps, in a tavern. But, as with any community, when there was enough wealth and an established elite, they set out to build a proper building. The committee approved the project in the spring of 1769 and made the specifications available for inspection at the Raleigh tavern. When, two years later, the undertaker (we don't know his name) turned over the building, Williamsburg had a court house with all the proper symbols of permanence and authority. It had large compass headed windows, imposing doors, solid construction, and a high cupola for all to see. We know little of what the interior looked like, however; it was gutted by fire in 1911.

But what of Mourning Richards, the unfortunate undertaker of Aquia? He was an important builder in the area with a number of projects underway at the time of the church disaster. Were he to go bankrupt, several prominent members of the community also would lose their investments. He appealed to the public for relief; to the vestry and the House of Burgesses. They bailed him out, (the public has deep pockets) and he rebuilt the church as it stands to this day.

ROY UNDERHILL
MASTER HOUSEWRIGHT
COLONIAL WILLIAMSBURG

Churches in Eight American Colonies

Text by
Hobart B. Upjohn
Photographs by
Kenneth Clark
Originally published in 1929 as White Pine Monograph
Volume XV, Number 1

Detail of Portico
ST. PHILIP'S CHURCH — 1835 — CHARLESTON, SOUTH CAROLINA

CHURCHES IN EIGHT AMERICAN COLONIES

WHEN Wren introduced the Classic interpretation of the English Gothic spire, he little realized what its influence would be. Many of the properties of the Churches which he was rebuilding were fixed by lot, foundations and established and fixed custom. The people of London were, as the English are today, quite set in their habits. They did not care to change and we read how they were unwilling to give up their old sites for a better plan of the city submitted by Wren. It is little wonder then, that Wren was faced with the problem of remaining faithful to the new found styles and at the same time meeting the requirements and prejudices of the congregation. Out of this apparently unsolvable condition of affairs grew a new flower, to be added to the master styles of the past.

The designs, however, were for the most part built in masonry material throughout—a fact so many times lost sight of. Naturally, therefore, the mouldings and detail had to be kept coarse and big and where spires were finished with plain surfaces, panels were introduced in marble. So also many other details were the result of meeting conditions of material and custom beyond the control of the designer.

The great fire of London occurred in 1666. Sir Christopher Wren was then thirty-four years old and it appears from history that architectural practice was not very different in those days than it is today. Wren was the first man, practically, on the job to submit a new plan for the city and got the work through his promptness and alertness. This was in the middle of the English Renaissance. Inigo Jones had already implanted his mark upon the architecture of England and it is not surprising that Wren, having already been retained to rebuild the city, should come forward and take the prominent part in its development.

Wren built a great number of churches in England and it is remarkable how really little of our Colonial architecture is drawn from or based upon Wren's designs. There appears to be a popular superstition that Wren was the inspirer of our colonial churches. I am convinced that we must look elsewhere for the real true inspiration.

When you consider this country at the time of 1666, we were building very few structures, at least few which remain today. The Witches' house in Salem and a series of houses of that type extending along the coast around Boston and here and there about the country a few odd buildings are the only evidence of that time. Wren was nearly seventy years old at the opening of the eighteenth century and there are very few church buildings whose dates extend back beyond that time.

Moreover, Wren's designs were largely in stone, more or less heavy and decidedly a transition from the Gothic to the Renaissance. It is astonishing how many of his spires are strongly influenced by the Gothic predecessors. A few suggest our colonial churches. St. Bride's in Fleet Street—St. Mary le Bow, St. Vedast, Foster Lane, and a few others may have had their influence. St. Peter's, Cornhill, may have possibly been responsible for many peculiar designs as well.

It is more than likely however, that James Gibbs, who was born in 1682 and died in 1754, was really the inspirer of the American Colonial. The churches of St. Martin's-in-the-Field and St. Mary le Strand have sufficient suggestion of the colonial inspiration to justify such an assertion. Moreover, in 1728 Gibbs published a book of designs of churches in London and it is astonishing to look through it and see how very much of the colonial inspiration is indicated in these designs. The designs, of course, were all made on the basis of using stone or marble, and for this reason it will be easily recognized that the detail is much more severe than in our colonial work. In our country we did not have the means to cut very deep mullions. The use of wood instead of stone varied the size and shape of the mouldings and the difference in the method of construction was responsible for a much lighter and more delicate style being evolved. The American Renaissance or colonial is unmistakably different from its English ancestors. It is most interesting to see how various parts of the country have adopted different elements of design. For example, there is a peculiar type of domically completed tower in and around Richmond which quite evidently comes from the Gibbs designs modified to meet our American conditions. The design of Wren's nearest to this type was St. Peter's, Cornhill, built in 1681, but it is not a design sufficiently related to our colonial to be taken as influencing the work here. We have with this chapter a number of most delightful churches in America of this period and I have arranged them according to a sequence in design.

St. Paul's, Edenton, North Carolina, is one of the most picturesque of the very early American churches. Edenton was the scene of a second protest tea party and it is very proud of their part in the War for Independence. In front of the old Court House there extends to the bay a great green on which stands a fence-post holding the tea pot.

This church was built in 1736. Its length is sixty feet, its width 40' 3" and its height 18' 6" while the thickness of the walls is 2' 6". The bricks are 2½" x 3¾" x 8½" and may have been imported, as Edenton is a seaport town. The brick is laid in Flemish bond.

The tower and spire are unusual—while colonial it reflects the Gothic spires of England. The church follows the custom of the Anglican Church and has its chancel toward the east. As in many colonial churches, it has side doors quite as prominent as at the west. These doors are the more used because the tower door is toward the inside of the lot.

St. Paul's, Eastchester, N.Y., erected 1768, is one of the very interesting churches of the Renaissance revival in this country. It is interesting to note how the original builders found it necessary to economize on cut stone for the entire body of the church. Brick is used as a substitute wherever cut stone would be required as quoins and trim around the openings. The sills of windows and the two moulded courses are of stone, but in the belfry cut stone is used entirely. The design with its spire-like roof reflects the pure Renaissance of England.

There is a calm and restful simplicity in the design. The severe shaft of native split stone serves as a strong and dignified support to a belfry which on any lighter base would appear too heavy.

Trinity Church at Swedesboro, New Jersey. Built 1784. This section was largely settled by Swedes who are responsible for several beautiful churches—Gloria Dei in Philadelphia being one of the most prominent. The church at Swedesboro is one of the largest.

Taken apart, the design might be a court house or town hall to which is attached a tower of five distinct

stories. It has two side doors to the east and west, the church not being orientated as at Edenton. Another peculiarity is that the tower is on the opposite end from the main entrance in the south. Its severe simplicity is not without charm and appeal. The surfaces of the spire are made with matched boards to produce an unbroken effect and its motives are accentuated by means of the slight pilasters flanking them and by the pilasters at the corners. The tower and spire were added in 1838.

But it is in the details that the church excels. It is to be regretted that we have not a photograph of its southern front where can be seen a well designed Palladian window, but we fortunately have a splendid photograph of the south door. Here it will be seen the brick are laid in Flemish bond. The paneled doors are flanked with two delicately fluted Doric columns. The architrave, frieze and cornice carry out the full order in exquisite taste. Even the soffit of the overhang is decorated with a colonial pattern of strap work, reminiscent of the Jacobean, charmingly worked in.

The front doors are made with three panels to each door while on the side the doors have four panels each. There is a delightful refinement suggested in the arrangement of the panels. Notice that the space of the middle panel of the side doors is taken up by a broad rail on the front door, no doubt to accommodate the lock. The side door shows no hardware and is probably secured by bolts from the inside—an economy of a lock in days when locks were made by hand.

The First Congregational Church at Lebanon, Conn. This church was built in 1807—the outgrowth of the colonial. Look at the details of the tower closely and you will see that the design is essentially made to be carried out in wood. The panels of the spire are made by planting on mouldings. The pilasters, urns, railing, cornices are all fine, delicate and appropriate for wood.

The church is built of brick, painted. It faces southeast, perhaps so that large windows on the sides of clear glass would not produce too much glare during the morning service. The tower and spire are what attract our greatest attention. The clock is placed in the belfry chamber and the question arises whether it was really in the mind of the architect when he designed the tower or if it was put in as an afterthought, perhaps a detail added after his work was done, for it does not tie into the rest of the design. The probabilities are that this was originally intended to be an open belfry. The low black hole is quite disfiguring, but the delicate spire is delightful in its proportions and detail.

The Church at Wethersfield, Conn. This church has as its basic principal the same general motives of the church in Swedesboro, N.J.—three rectangular stories

ST. PAUL'S CHURCH—1736—EDENTON, NORTH CAROLINA

Detail of Steeple
ST. PAUL'S CHURCH, EASTCHESTER, NEW YORK

ST. PAUL'S CHURCH—1768—EASTCHESTER, NEW YORK

but each carefully proportioned. The use of spirelets, flanked on the four sides with delicate urns on the four corners of the first story is most unusual and yet the detail tends to soften down the transition from the large rectangular base to the first story of the spire. These spirelets are reminiscent of the tall pinnacles of a Gothic spire and architecturally serve the same purpose.

The charming lantern at the top gives lightness to the design, while placing the bells in the main body of the tower, which is of brick, is most logical. The desire for an open story is here shown, though the architect seems to have reinforced the design by bringing the lantern base through the lower story. Another unusual feature is the use of a double set of urns around the lantern; a feature bidding to lighten the design and increase its verticality. These details have greatly added to the unity and growth of the spire in a most pleasing manner. A careful comparison of this spire with Trinity Church, Newport, leads one to believe that they were by the same hand. The two are almost identical except for the towers on which they stand.

The First Congregational Church at Old Bennington, Vt. This church is dated as 1806. The use of rounded edged clapboards is interesting. The front doors with the heavy raised mouldings and each door two panels, and especially the paneled transom of the central front door, lead one to suspect an alteration in this part of the building, but with the date 1806 it is likely the influence of the new changes in architectural design.

The use of the open story in the spire is a bold endeavor at original design. This may be well considered as of purely American origin for such a design is impossible of execution in any other material than wood; the use of wood being largely confined to this side of the water. The columns structurally no doubt run through to the cornice and are strongly braced by the arches below the frieze. They are subject to quite a bending stress due to wind, a stress which would be impossible to provide against were they of stone.

The glazed lantern reflects the taste of James Gibbs and may be remotely descended from his designs. The elongating of this story and the use of elliptical windows adds a charm to the whole design. This church doubtless was the inspiration of the Congregational Church built at Manchester by the Sea, Mass., in 1809, and may have been by the same architect.

The Congregational Church at Haverhill, N.H. The mass relation of the front to the tower is good, although open to the criticism of double composition and a tendency to fall apart due to the two large flanking windows.

Were the church in Europe one would account for the doors through the symbolic representation of the dual nature of Christ. Perhaps the church was largely influenced by Quakers, whose custom it was to separate the sexes. Another weak feature is the use of two skewbacks on a Palladian window without completing the structural support. On the whole, however, the design is sturdy and assuring. The church faces south, no attention being paid to orthodox orientation.

The Fifth Meeting House, Lancaster, Mass. This church, shown on page 29, is the work of Charles Bulfinch. It is most interesting to see the master hand of this architect coming out in the handling of the various details of the church. An inherent massiveness independent of the influence of other architects preceding him, although there is the possibility that the dome might have been suggested, but it's entirely independent swing, its belfry modified somewhat from the Temple of Vesta, it's shafts mounting up to the central portion of the tower and the massive treatment of the front porch, are all characteristic of an architect whose work has stood and been admired for many years by architects of our country.

The church was built in 1816 of Lancaster brick and timber and the lime came from Bolton, Mass. Here again we see a church which faces almost south and it seems to be a characteristic of the meeting house of New England to be placed in this position. It is probable that the axial relation to the lot was adopted for the reason that they used clear glass in those days and the glare in the windows from east and west was disagreeable, the morning service usually occurring about 10:30. For the most part, the light was away from directly shining in the side windows as it would be if the church were built according to the established orientation.

Turning now to the heavily built front porch with its great arches made with a single rowlock, there is a delicacy of design combined with strength that is pleasing and unusual. The finish of the belfry with its six openings and alternate blanks between the columns is most attractive and the incorporating of the little band of festoons around the top of the belfry adds a touch characteristic of the architect.

St. Philip's Church, Charleston, South Carolina, shown in the two accompanying photographs, is nearer to the heavy bold architecture of Sir Christopher Wren. The tower and spire are built up stories of solid stone and the detail is characteristically heavy in the use of its stone throughout.

On the porches again the great strength of its material is apparent. The spire is unusually high and almost questionably heavy for the church itself. This design lacks the fine delicacy of the other colonial work.

TRINITY CHURCH—1784—SWEDESBORO, NEW JERSEY
Tower and spire built 1838.

Detail of Front Door
TRINITY CHURCH, SWEDESBORO, NEW JERSEY

FIRST CONGREGATIONAL CHURCH—1807—LEBANON, CONNECTICUT

CHURCH AT WETHERSFIELD, CONNECTICUT

Detail of Pulpit
FIRST PRESBYTERIAN CHURCH, TENNENT, NEW JERSEY

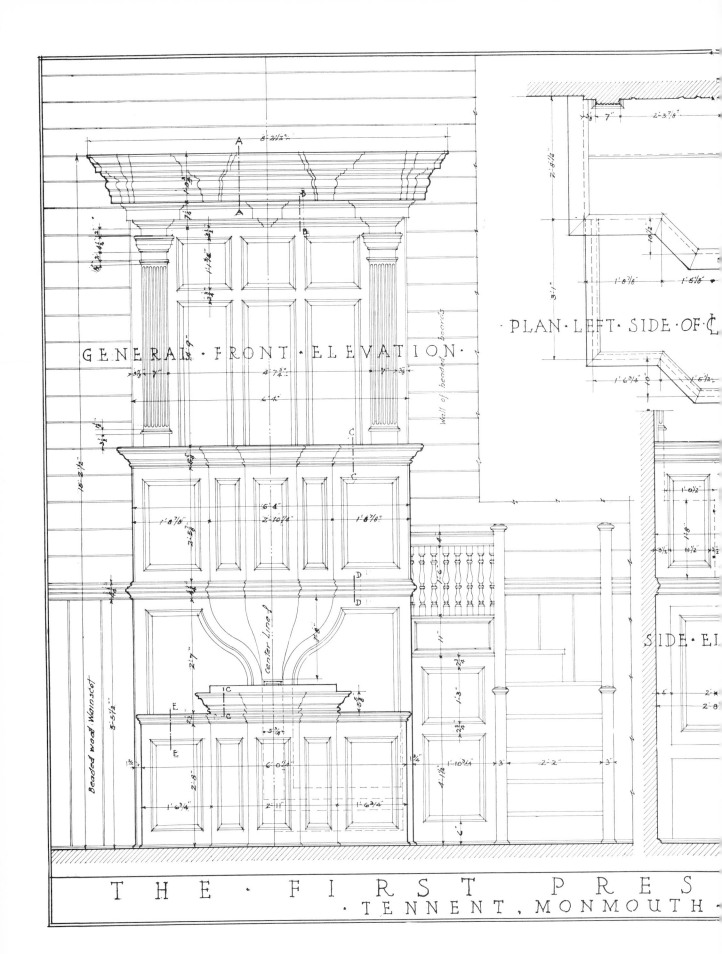

GENERAL · FRONT · ELEVATION ·

PLAN · LEFT · SIDE · OF · C

SIDE · EL

Beaded wood Wainscot

Wall of beaded boards

center Line

THE · FIRST · PRES
· TENNENT, MONMOUTH ·

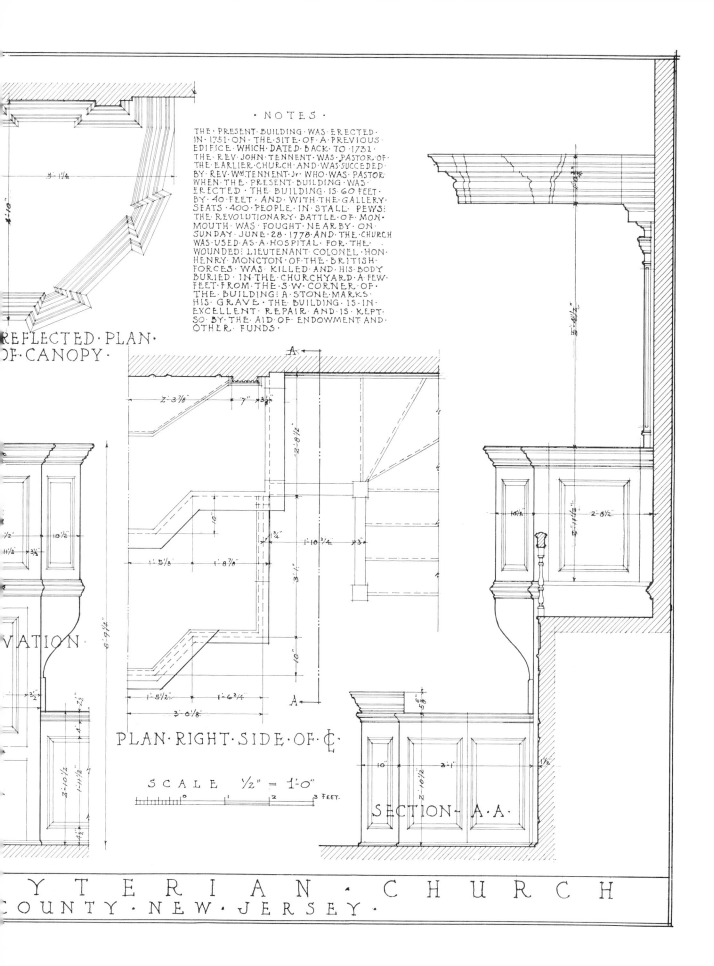

REFLECTED · PLAN ·
OF · CANOPY ·

PLAN · RIGHT · SIDE · OF · ℄

SCALE ½" = 1'·0"

0   1   2   3 FEET.

VATION

SECTION · A · A ·

YTERIAN · CHURCH
COUNTY · NEW · JERSEY ·

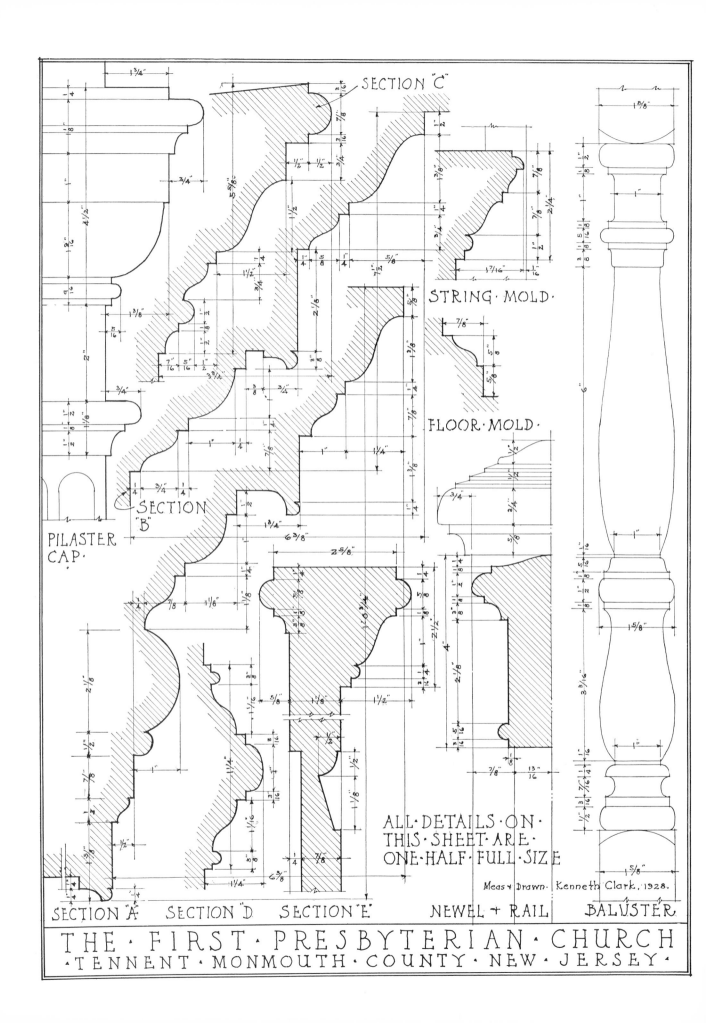

SECTION "C"

STRING · MOLD ·

FLOOR · MOLD ·

PILASTER
CAP·

SECTION
"B"

SECTION "A"   SECTION "D"   SECTION "E"   NEWEL + RAIL   BALUSTER

ALL·DETAILS·ON·
THIS·SHEET·ARE·
ONE·HALF·FULL·SIZE

Meas + Drawn. Kenneth Clark, 1928.

THE · FIRST · PRESBYTERIAN · CHURCH
·TENNENT · MONMOUTH · COUNTY · NEW · JERSEY·

North Elevation
FIRST PRESBYTERIAN CHURCH — 1751 — TENNENT, NEW JERSEY

CONGREGATIONAL CHURCH, HAVERHILL, NEW HAMPSHIRE

FIRST CONGREGATIONAL CHURCH — 1806 — OLD BENNINGTON, VERMONT

Detail of Spire
FIRST CONGREGATIONAL CHURCH — 1806 — OLD BENNINGTON, VERMONT

Detail of Cupola
FIFTH MEETING HOUSE — 1816 — LANCASTER, MASSACHUSETTS

ST. PHILIP'S CHURCH—1835—CHARLESTON, SOUTH CAROLINA

Early Boston Churches

Text by
Frank Chouteau Brown
Photographs by
Arthur C. Haskell
Originally published in 1937 as White Pine Monograph
Volume XXIII, Number 6

CHRIST CHURCH (OLD NORTH)—1723—BOSTON, MASSACHUSETTS
Seen from the Prado Park. The church faces on Salem Street in the North End.

EARLY BOSTON CHURCHES

S UBSTANTIALLY all the early settlements of the Massachusetts Bay Colony were motivated from a religious background. In most cases the group of settlers was composed of a congregation and its pastor, and the cause of their emigration was usually a desire to conduct their ritual of Sabbath Day worship from an individual angle, or to maintain a theological belief that might vary in what we would probably now consider a very minor particular from the generally established form. While practically all the early Puritan and Pilgrim settlers were desirous of divorcing themselves entirely from all the forms and ritual of the established Church of England.

So, too, the everyday control of each community group—no matter what might be its relation to the chartering authority behind it—remained restricted to the members of the church congregation forming its nucleus, as members of the church alone had the privilege of the temporal vote. In some part this was a natural outgrowth of the method they had been following in the mother country—where they had been accustomed to use the body of the parish church for all community occasions—town meetings as well as purely social gatherings.

If one of the New World communities happened to be composed of two congregations, with more than one minister, it was a matter of only a short time before the groups separated, and each minister would become the center of his own congregational settlement. Sometimes the removal of one group would be made en masse; sometimes it was gradual, a few first going on ahead and selecting the new site for settlement; to which the others would then remove, as opportunity or convenience gave occasion. Much of New England was thus enlarged and settled within the first score of years after the landing.

And thus also it came naturally about that, as soon as the settlers had provided themselves with shelter, they immediately turned to erecting a structure which would serve the purposes of both town house and church. It is therefore usually referred to in their records as the "meeting house" or church; for as such it would serve all necessary uses of the town house, —which usually was not built until later in the history of the community. As an example, one might point to the "Oldest Town Hall in Continuous Use in New England"—the little known meeting house erected in 1743 by Scotch Presbyterian emigrants, four years after their arrival at Pelham, in the western part of the state, a structure that is still in use as the town hall, though the church meetings have been transferred to a newer Neo-Greek (1839) church building.

And, most fortunately, Boston still has a number of old churches that comprise a truly notable group. In number, in age, in their architectural beauty, variety in design, and historical associations, they are unrivaled in this country and are only approached in interest by those similar structures surviving from the same early periods in Philadelphia.

Oldest and most popular among them is the Old North (Christ Church, Boston) on Salem Street, in what is generally known as the North End of the city. It was built in 1723, and has been continuously in use as a house of worship since that time—with the exception of the brief period when the British troops occupied the city during the first years of the Revolution. Next oldest is the Old South Meeting House, on Washington and Milk streets, which dates from 1729, but has of recent years (since about 1880) been used only as an historical museum, for educational purposes and the meetings of a community forum.

Next follows King's Chapel on Tremont Street, the present structure, built in 1749; St. Stephen's (built originally as the New North, 1804) on Hanover Street, North End; West Church, Cambridge Street, 1806; the Abolition Church, Smith Court, Beacon Hill, 1806; Charles St. A. M. E. Church, 1807; Park Street Church, corner Tremont, 1809; and St. Paul's the Episcopal Cathedral Church, also on Tremont Street, built in 1820 from designs by Alexander Parris. The last of the walls of the Hollis Street Church, 1810, have come down only within the past year—and the brownstone Arlington Street Church, corner of Boylston Street, 1860, has a distinguished appearance, hardly to be expected of its comparatively late date, but probably resulting from having been rather closely based upon late Renaissance London church models.

And this list covers only the downtown edifices in the old Boston area; it does not include the several other historic structures remaining in Roxbury, Dorchester, Charlestown (all now parts of Boston), the immediately adjoining cities of Brookline and Cambridge—nor others nearby, which would easily increase the total by at least a half-dozen more!

cliffe arrived in Boston on the *Rose*, May 15, 1686.

A request for the use of one of the three Congregational meeting houses for the English church services having been refused, they were offered instead the library room in the east end of the old Town House, and the first Episcopal service was held there, on June 15, 1686, using a "movable pulpit," and table at one end with benches or "formes" set up along the sides of the room, facing to the center. (This was the original arrangement of Holden Chapel, 1744, at Harvard in Cambridge.) In the New England meeting house the pulpit was usually placed midway along one

Box Pews

CHRIST CHURCH—1723—BOSTON, MASSACHUSETTS

Two of these old edifices were built for the Church of England, assisted by the Society for the Propagation of the Gospel in Foreign Parts—which represented all that the early settlers of this area had crossed the sea to avoid! Already the Puritans had persecuted the Quakers for heresy—although they had begun to worship as early as 1677—and in 1697 they built on Brattle Street the first brick meeting house in Boston. Meanwhile the Baptists—equally heretical from the narrow Puritan point-of-view—had built a Boston house of worship, in 1680. And in 1679 some residents of Boston first petitioned the King for a Church of England; and, in answer to this plea, the Reverend Robert Rat-

side, facing toward the principal door, opposite. There were often doors at the two ends of the building, as well. The early benches were placed along all the walls, facing toward the center. Later "box pews" were built about the four sides of the room; then gradually filled in the floor area, leaving only three or four benches facing the pulpit along the very front of the space. Sometimes the stairways to the galleries were placed in the two forward corners of the main room, and sometimes they were contained in two-story vestibules at the ends; while a little later, one of these end vestibules might develop externally into a tower—as in the familiar example furnished by the Old South.

CHRIST CHURCH (OLD NORTH) — 1723 — BOSTON, MASSACHUSETTS

Detail of Pulpit
CHRIST CHURCH (OLD NORTH) — 1723 — BOSTON, MASSACHUSETTS

KING'S CHAPEL—1749—CORNER TREMONT AND SCHOOL STREETS, BOSTON, MASSACHUSETTS

The granite building designed by Peter Harrison. Portico added in 1789, claimed by
some to have been designed by Charles Bulfinch. Old pulpit shown on pages 39–41
was removed from the wooden building, on same site, and completed in 1754.

In the Church of England, the pulpit was always at
the chancel (east) end of the church, located either
at one side the center (as in the Old North) or in
the middle (as at Trinity, 1726, Newport, Rhode Island).
The benches in the galleries were continued for a considerable length of time, especially when slaves were
accommodated in one portion.

Pews were introduced in England during the reign
of Charles II, as a great luxury. Sir Christopher Wren
originally objected to them in his London churches.
In the earliest examples they were built by the holder
in each case, but they had become a regular part of

church equipment by the end of Queen Anne's reign.

A wooden church building was erected on the present site of King's Chapel, at a cost of £284 16s.
($1381.24), and first used on June 30, 1689. The
pews were not added until 1694, when "railed" pews,
with an upper space filled with small turned balusters,
were built, at a cost of £53. The wooden church was
enlarged by 1714, and a clock was then received from
"the Brittish Society," which took the place of the
mounted hourglass, which had formerly stood beside
the preacher. Pews were reassigned to the proprietors,
each paying for the building of his own; which were

now "built in one forme without banisters." A small organ, brought from London, was also received from Thos. Brattle, Esq., Treasurer of Harvard College.

By the time of the Reformation, the high pulpit, with six or eight ornamented sides, had supplanted the old portable box desk. The pulpit was added to King's Chapel in 1717, at a cost of £36 13s.; and was removed to the new building, after it was completed, in 1753 — from which time may also date the sound-

erected, and the portico was finally added in 1789 — some claim from designs of Bulfinch. The old organ was supplanted by another in 1756. The first Episcopal Church in New England, it continued of that denomination until 1785, when it became the first Unitarian Church in the United States.

At the time the granite King's Chapel was built, both the present Christ Church and Old South buildings were in existence. The records of Christ Church

Balcony
KING'S CHAPEL — 1749 — BOSTON, MASSACHUSETTS
Designed by Peter Harrison.

ing board and, perhaps, the pulpit stairs. The present King's Chapel building was built of Quincy granite blocks, in 1749, from plans by Peter Harrison, who had come to this country, with Smibert and others, accompanying Bishop Berkeley when he arrived intending to found a college, in 1728. A pupil of Sir John Vanbrough, he assisted his brother as a merchant in Newport, Rhode Island. Originally intended to be built with a stone tower and spire, the spire was never

contain a carpentry estimate by Thomas Tippen and Thomas Bennett, master-builders, both being Church Proprietors, for £396:16:10, and show that 15 shillings was paid for a "stone," laid April 15, 1723. The church, still unfinished, was used on December 29 of that same year. No bills for any plans of the church have been found, except one of March 26, 1741, from William Price, for "Designing & Drawing Sundry Drafts for ye new Spire" of £17:10, against which was

KING'S CHAPEL—1749—TREMONT AND SCHOOL STREETS, BOSTON, MASSACHUSETTS
Pulpit added to King's Chapel in 1717.

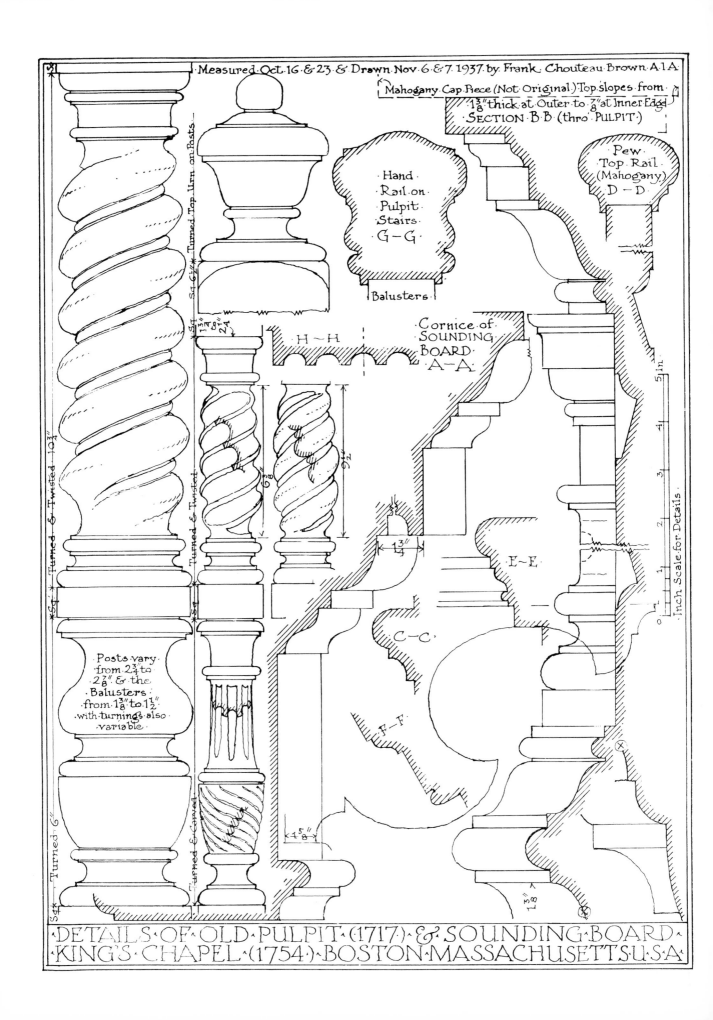

Measured Oct. 16 & 23 & Drawn Nov. 6 & 7. 1937. by Frank Chouteau Brown A.I.A.

Mahogany Cap Piece (Not Original) Top slopes from 1⅜" thick at Outer to ⅞" at Inner Edge. SECTION B-B (thro' PULPIT)

Pew Top Rail (Mahogany) D-D

Hand Rail on Pulpit Stairs G-G

Balusters

Cornice of SOUNDING BOARD A-A

H-H

E-E

C-C

F-F

Inch Scale for Details.

Turned & Twisted 10¾"   Sq.   Turned Top Urn on Posts   Sq. 6¼"

Sq.   Turned & Twisted   Sq.   Turned & Carved

Turned 6"

Posts vary from 2¾" to 2⅞" & the Balusters from 1⅜" to 1½" with turnings also variable.

DETAILS OF OLD PULPIT (1717) & SOUNDING BOARD KING'S CHAPEL (1754) BOSTON MASSACHUSETTS U.S.A

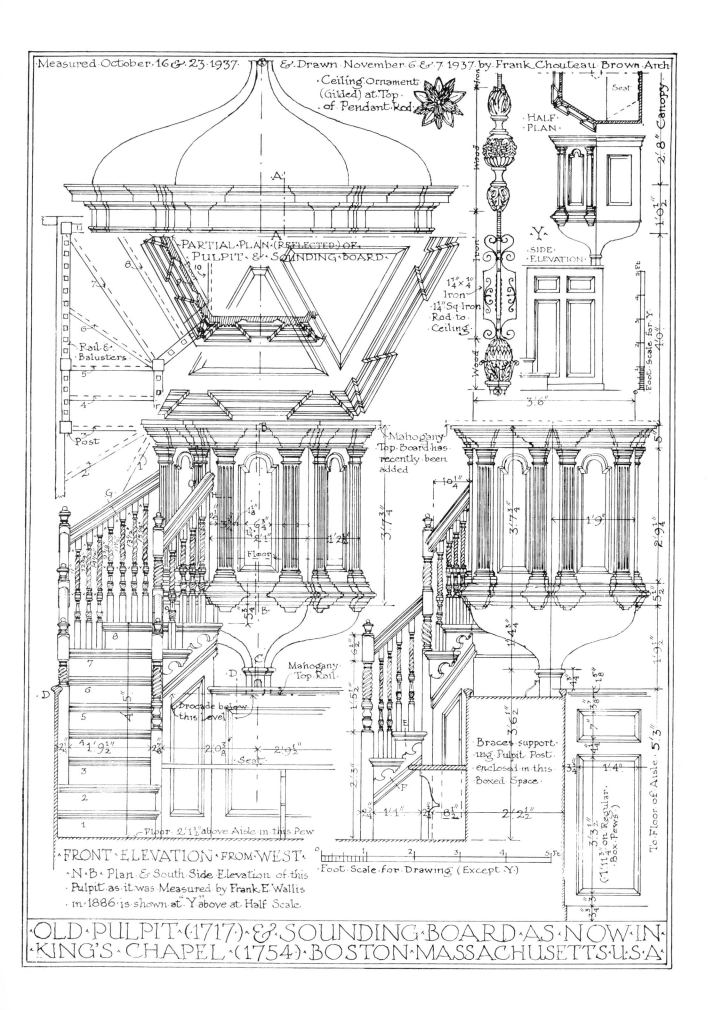

Measured October 16 & 23 1937 & Drawn November 6 & 7 1937 by Frank Chouteau Brown Arch

Ceiling Ornament (Gilded) at Top of Pendant Rod

HALF PLAN

Seat

2' 8" Canopy

1' 0½"

PARTIAL PLAN (REFLECTED) OF PULPIT & SOUNDING BOARD

A

Rail & Balusters

Post

Y

SIDE ELEVATION

1¼" × ¼" Iron

1¼" Sq. Iron Rod to Ceiling

3' 6"

4' 0"

Foot Scale for Y

Mahogany Top Board has recently been added

Mahogany Top Rail

3' 4¾"

3' 7¾"

1' 9"

2' 9¼"

10¼"

1' 2¼"

18"

6¾"

5¾"

4' 1"

Floor

5' 2"

1' 9½"

1' 4¾"

4¾"

1' 8"

3' 6½"

Braces supporting Pulpit Post enclosed in this Boxed Space

To Floor of Aisle · 5' 3"

Brocade below this Level

Seat

2' 0⅜"

2' 9½"

G

D

6

5

4

3

2

1

8

7

2¼"

1' 9½"

2¾"

Floor 2' 1½" above Aisle in this Pew

2' 3"

1' 5½"

1' 5½"

6½"

2¼"

1' 1"

2¾"

8½"

2' 2½"

7"

3⅜"

1' 4"

4½"

3' 3½"

(1' 11¾" on Regular Box Pews)

·FRONT·ELEVATION·FROM·WEST·

·N·B· Plan & South Side Elevation of this Pulpit as it was Measured by Frank E. Wallis in 1886 is shown at "Y" above at Half Scale.

0 · Foot Scale for Drawing (Except Y)

·OLD·PULPIT·(1717)·&·SOUNDING·BOARD·AS·NOW·IN· KING'S·CHAPEL·(1754)·BOSTON·MASSACHUSETTS·U·S·A·

Interior
KING'S CHAPEL — 1749 — BOSTON, MASSACHUSETTS

offset "To my subscription to ye spire £20." The same bill provided for a payment to "Mr. John Indecott" who built the wooden portion of tower and spire, in a pasture nearby, it being raised whole into position in 1740, at which time the upper brick story of the tower was also added. The weathervane, by Deacon Shem Drowne, who made the grasshopper on Faneuil Hall, the India vane on Province House, etc., was in place and hoisted with it.

This steeple was blown down in the great storm of October, 1804, and was replaced from Bulfinch's design, 175 feet high, (16 feet shorter than the original — though otherwise very like it!), although no bill for his services has been found. William Price was a printseller and mapmaker (famous early "prospect" of Boston bearing his name) and may have brought, on one of his many trips from London, builder's handbooks showing Wren designs, which may have been copied for this church.

The Old South Church was begun March 31, 1729 and the first service was held April 27, 1730. The in-

side was entirely destroyed in 1775, by the 17th regiment of British dragoons, who were allowed to use the building as a riding school. It was repaired in 1782. It has two sets of galleries, of the Tuscan and Doric orders, with a later pulpit ornamented with Corinthian columns. The steeple is 180 feet high, and still contains the original clock works.

The first West Church was a wooden building of 1737 with a high spire, which was destroyed by the British. The present building was erected in 1806, from designs by Asher Benjamin. It had a very handsome mahogany pulpit, which was removed to the Meeting House Hill Church in Dorchester, when it was taken over as a branch library about thirty-five years ago. The original balcony and clock remain.

The comparative rarity of existing church designs by Charles Bulfinch lends an exceptional interest to St. Stephen's Church on Hanover Street in the North End. Of no less than ten ecclesiastical edifices, reputed to have been from his designs; only three now remain. One, built at Pittsfield in 1789, has been

ST. STEPHEN'S CHURCH—1804—HANOVER STREET, BOSTON, MASSACHUSETTS
Designed by Charles Bulfinch as the "New North" Church.

through many changes, and is at this very time, going through another. The well known church at Lancaster, built in 1817, considered his best as well as his last (excepting the church in Washington of 1822 — demolished 1900 — and the apocryphal, though still standing, Peterborough, New Hampshire, edifice of 1825) is the only one that has been comparatively carefully conserved. In Boston there remains but one of the authentic five he built in that city; now known as St. Stephen's, which is celebrating on November 21 of this year the diamond jubilee of its consecration for Catholic use. It was built in 1804 as the "New North" Church, on the site of an earlier wooden building of 1714, from designs by Bulfinch; who had, the very year previous, designed the Catholic Holy Cross Church (formerly at the foot of the Tontine Crescent on Franklin Street).

At the widening of Hanover Street, some years ago, this building was moved back, some changes made in the approach to the main doorway, and new doors opened on each side of the projecting vestibule. Upon the interior, the balconies remain practically as designed, but the whole altar end was rebuilt. Within the last two years, an open park, known as the Prado has been made by demolition, that extends from the opposite side of Hanover Street way through to Unity Street, just at the rear of the Old North, providing an unobstructed view of St. Stephen's façade. The present top of the tower has also been changed since the original finial was affected by lightning, years ago.

Park Street Church — once known as Brimstone Corner — was designed by Peter Banner, an English architect, in 1809. He began to practice as an architect, in Boston, at 29 Orange Street, in 1806; and was also architect in charge of the Bunker Hill Monument, in 1825. He was assisted by Solomon Willard, first as a carver executing the capitals on the spire of the Park Street Church; and who also later, in 1816, made the panels on the David Sears House at 42 Beacon Street (now used as the Somerset Club). Willard was also associated with Alexander Parris.

Balconies

ST. STEPHEN'S CHURCH — 1804 — HANOVER STREET, BOSTON, MASSACHUSETTS
Designed by Charles Bulfinch as the "New North" Church.

Altar End
ST. STEPHEN'S CHURCH, HANOVER STREET, BOSTON, MASSACHUSETTS
Rebuilt in connection with auditions at back of building.

PARK STREET CHURCH—1809—CORNER TREMONT STREET, BOSTON, MASSACHUSETTS
Designed by Peter Banner, assisted by Solomon Willard.

Country Meeting Houses

Text by
Robert P. Bellows
Photographs by
Kenneth Clark

Originally published in 1925 as White Pine Monograph
Volume XI, Number 5

FIRST PARISH CHURCH—1809—ASHBY, MASSACHUSETTS

COUNTRY MEETING HOUSES ALONG THE MASSACHUSETTS-NEW HAMPSHIRE LINE

ALONG the middle part of the northern boundary of Massachusetts is a cluster of country meeting houses. They are situated in the southwest corner of New Hampshire and across the line in Massachusetts, in the townships of Ashby, Templeton, Fitzwilliam, Westmoreland, and Acworth Town (near S. Acworth, New Hampshire.)

Built at the beginning of the last century these simple structures are remarkable for the richness and originality of their exterior detail and ornament. They show the wooden country meeting house of a hundred or more years ago at its best.

In many ways they are very similar. They all are set on high ground, fronting on village greens, with their backs to open meadow or woodland and, in two cases, a country graveyard. They can be seen from afar off and dominate, by bulk and height, each composition of town and landscape.

In size they vary from 50 to 58 feet in width, and between 60 and 68 feet in length. This does not include the porch or other motive on the front which in no case projects more than a few feet. At the rear they are square without projections. Each has a bell and an open belfry. Each is surmounted by a tower and an enormous weathervane. The more sophisticated carry the town clock.

Their builders placed them close to the ground with the land sloping away at the rear. Splendid big blocks of granite underpinning support the sills. Big granite slabs with generous treads rise gently in two or three steps to triple entrance doors.

The plans originally must have been much alike. At Templeton the congregation enters directly through a vestibule about 12 feet wide with stairs at each end leading to a gallery above and at each side. There is some evidence that the other churches were originally built in this fashion and that later they were floored over at the gallery level. This makes them now two-story buildings with offices and smaller rooms on the ground floor, though this is not apparent from the outside.

The windows are of the simple double-hung type with twenty-four lights, of the same character as house windows of the period. In proportion the openings are rectangles, in height about twice the width, which varies from 3 feet to 3 feet 6 inches. Three of the churches have eight windows on a side; the two shorter have six and five.

Templeton, built in 1811, is very, very like Fitzwilliam. The difference in length is a matter of inches; in width, some three feet. It is obvious that Fitzwilliam, built in 1817, was "taken almost straight" from Templeton.

Acworth Town also, built "about a hundred years ago," let us say in 1825, is almost identical with Fitzwilliam, except that it lacks the columnar porch and the clock and the steepled top. Thus did the fashions move up state. We have been able to compute from these three churches, their dates and distances, that in the early part of the nineteenth century, architectural styles traveled up country at the rate of about 2½ miles per year, a more conservative speed than at present.

In speaking severally of these old meeting houses, we like to refer to them *tout court* by the name of their towns alone. Thus architects are wont to speak reverentially of Chartres or Salisbury when they mean the great cathedrals in those delightful places. This use of "the container for the thing contained" is called metonymy by the learned. These gave, in the old days, as an example, that short yet pregnant phrase, "He drank the bottle." The meaning, except for the year and vintage, is perfectly clear.

ASHBY. Going north from Boston, we come first to Ashby. It is fittingly the earliest, built in 1809, and is a fine simple building, not unlike many other churches in the more immediate neighborhood of Boston. But the beauty of the trim of its triple door, the agreeable scale of its main cornice and the charm of its belfry tower make it one of the most satisfying of its type. The clapboarded Palladian window at the rear bespeaks by its position, the building was originally one-story.

To reach the other churches, we pass over a small

watershed and find the brooks now running with us to the westward. From that quarter must have come the new influences to be remarked in their architecture.

TEMPLETON, (good summer hotel), is but two years the junior of Ashby. But here we find new variations on the old tune. Hail to the Ionic order, see through the eyes of a country carpenter, Elias Carter, of Brimfield.

The wide columnar porch, the prototype of Fitz-william and Westmoreland, strikes a new though naive note. The intercolumniation follows more closely the proportions of a mantel motive, let us say, than those of classic precedent. The lintel is almost as long as the pediment. We would not have it otherwise. After all the porch is very shallow and the order very handsomely executed. Each of the four columns is carried on a pedestal, man high.

The main cornice is much like Ashby. It runs around the whole church. On the front is added an architrave and frieze. At the corners, Ionic pilasters run to the ground outdistancing the free columns by some six feet. It may be that these free columns once went the whole distance, then rotted at their base, and pedestals were substituted for their lower parts. In the porch pediment we find an elliptical window with palm "supporters."

FITZWILLIAM, (excellent old village tavern), is but fifteen miles to the northeast over the state line. Here we find the same order, cornices, balustrades, windows, doors and underpinning. The tower is almost identical. Painted elliptical "fake" windows at the top have been added and look surprisingly well. A pyramid at each corner of the main tower may well be of later date. The clock is placed somewhat lower, and there is a decorative panel beneath it. There is an engaging scoop in the soffit of the porch to enable a small Palladian window to make connections. The little elliptical window in the pediment has the crossed palm leaves. The building is now used entirely for town purposes.

The misfortunes, perseverance and final triumph of the townspeople in getting themselves a satisfactory church is well told in the Rev. Norton's Town History.

"In September of 1803, Thomas Stratton was paid three dollars and thirty cents for assisting to draft a plan for the meeting house.

"In 1816 a new and commodious meeting house was erected . . . at an expense of about seven thousand dollars which was a large sum for the people to raise at that time for such a purpose. This church . . . in every way a noble structure, like churches built about the same time in Athol, Templeton and Petersham."

(Note: Templeton alone exists today, in approximately its original form.)

"This church had been occupied for worship nine, or at most, ten Sabbaths, when during a thunder storm on the night of January 17, 1817, it was struck by lightning, fired and totally consumed. . . . The loss to the people was great, but it served the good purpose of uniting them as they had not been united for many years. . . . With slight changes in the foundations, the house now standing was erected. This church cost $6000." It was completed and dedicated "one year and twenty days," from the time of the catastrophe.

In this case, according to local traditions, the four big wooden columns were hewn into shape on the spot and hollowed out their entire length to avoid decay. Even then they were placed above the stone porch floor on strange granite blocks with chamfered corners.

WESTMORELAND, lies some twenty miles to the northwest. There are a few good old houses about a green, a charmingly placed old parsonage among them, no evident stores or post office—just a little hamlet, half-asleep.

Here we encounter the Tuscan Doric in all its New Hampshire glory. The white woodwork, the dark green blinds, the slate roof and the red cupola make a pleasant picture at the upper end of the sloping common. This church is the smallest, measuring but 50 by 60 feet. While the Ionic orders of Templeton and Fitz-william have a diameter of 2 feet, this Doric order is only 1 foot 6¾ inches. True to form, the shafts rest directly on raised granite blocks. The cornice is much simpler than the others.

The side windows on the top story must have been increased in size when the second floor was put in, all except the end ones at the top of the stairs. "False" blinds, which cover not only these small windows but also a large area of clapboard, are discreetly nailed shut for all time.

We sought information from pleasant people living at the foot of the green who, giving us the key, told us to be sure to climb the tower. This we did and beheld the silvery beauty of the Connecticut Valley. We mounted also the reading desk and there within the big Bible found what we wanted. In a delicate and clear script, "In September 1779 the first meeting was held in our present house of worship after its removal from the now called 'North Cemetery.' It cost to remove and fit up the building 2388 L. 11s. and 6d. . . . The house remained in this form until 1824 when an addition of 20 feet was put on the front, porches removed (sic) and a steeple added. . . . In 1853 it was remodelled into its present form."

This dates Westmoreland for our purpose as 1824.

The frame is earlier and the devastating second floor

CHURCH AT TEMPLETON, MASSACHUSETTS
Built in 1811 by Elias Carter.

must be the later "remodelling." But the fine belfry and front with their pleasing variations and simplifications were erected only seven years later than Fitzwilliam.

The cheerful manner in which this church was moved about is local legend. Destined for a site still farther from the "North Cemetery," it was held up *en route* by the astute tavernkeepers facing on the green who gave the movers a barrel of rum not to haul it further.

ACWORTH TOWN. If one has time it is well worth while stopping in Walpole to recuperate from such extensive globe trotting before motoring up to Acworth Town, a small settlement whose church is "as high as any in the state." It is a cross between Fitzwilliam and Ashby, but has arched triple doors. The tower, though much like its predecessors, is, to our thinking, the best of them all.

In these five meeting houses there is no note of the Greek Revival; rather the swan song of the later Colonial classic, sung by obscure rivals of Asher Benjamin. It is written that the late Charles F. McKim on seeing some of these churches expressed an admiration of their architecture.

Detail of Entablature
CHURCH AT TEMPLETON, MASSACHUSETTS

Detail of Spire
CHURCH AT TEMPLETON, MASSACHUSETTS

Detail of Spire
CHURCH AT FITZWILLIAM, NEW HAMPSHIRE

CHURCH — 1817 — FITZWILLIAM, NEW HAMPSHIRE

Doorway Cornice

Main Cornice

CHURCH AT FITZWILLIAM, NEW HAMPSHIRE

Detail of Spire
PARK HILL CHURCH, WESTMORELAND, NEW HAMPSHIRE

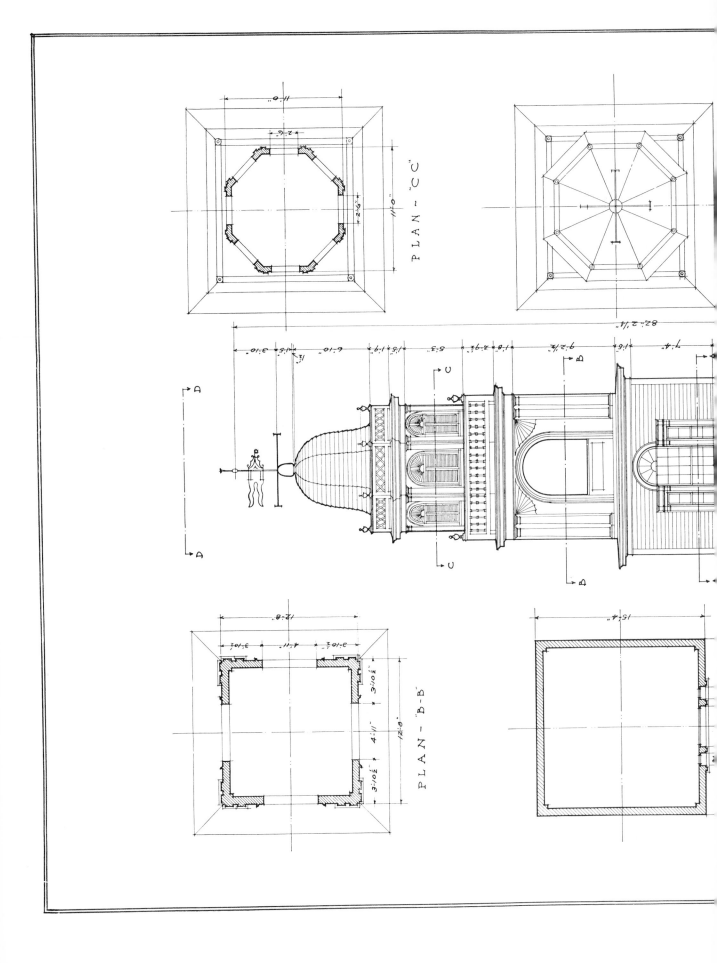

PLAN ~ "CC"

PLAN ~ "B-B"

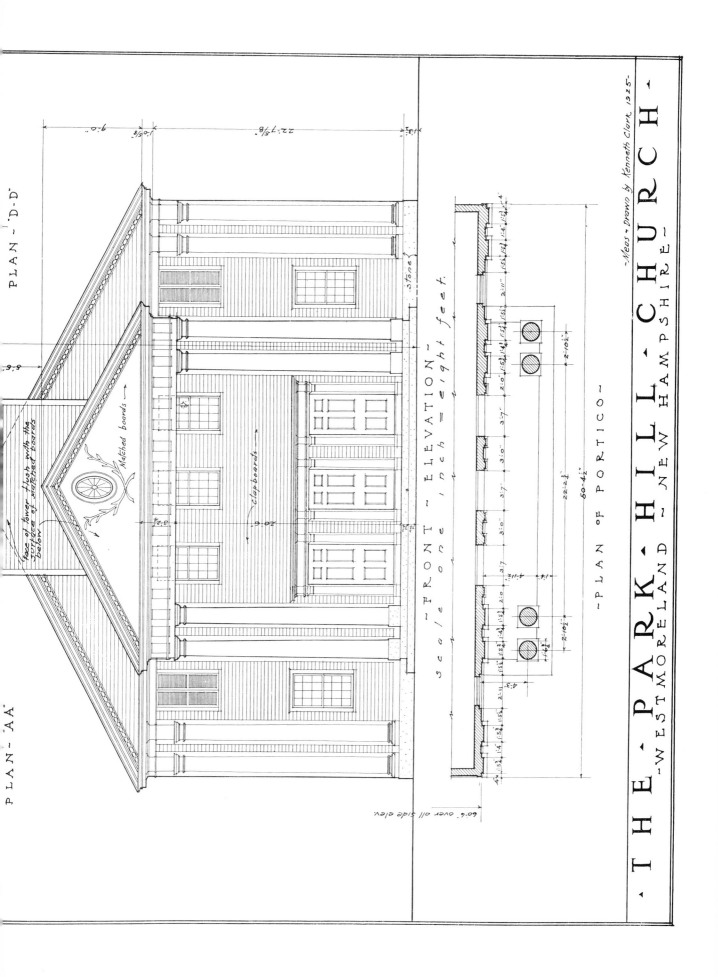

PLAN ~ "D·D"

PLAN ~ "AA"

~ FRONT ~ ELEVATION ~

scale one inch = eight feet

~ PLAN of PORTICO ~

· THE · PARK · HILL · CHURCH ·
~ WESTMORELAND ~ NEW HAMPSHIRE ~

~ Meas + Drawn by Kenneth Clark 1915 ~

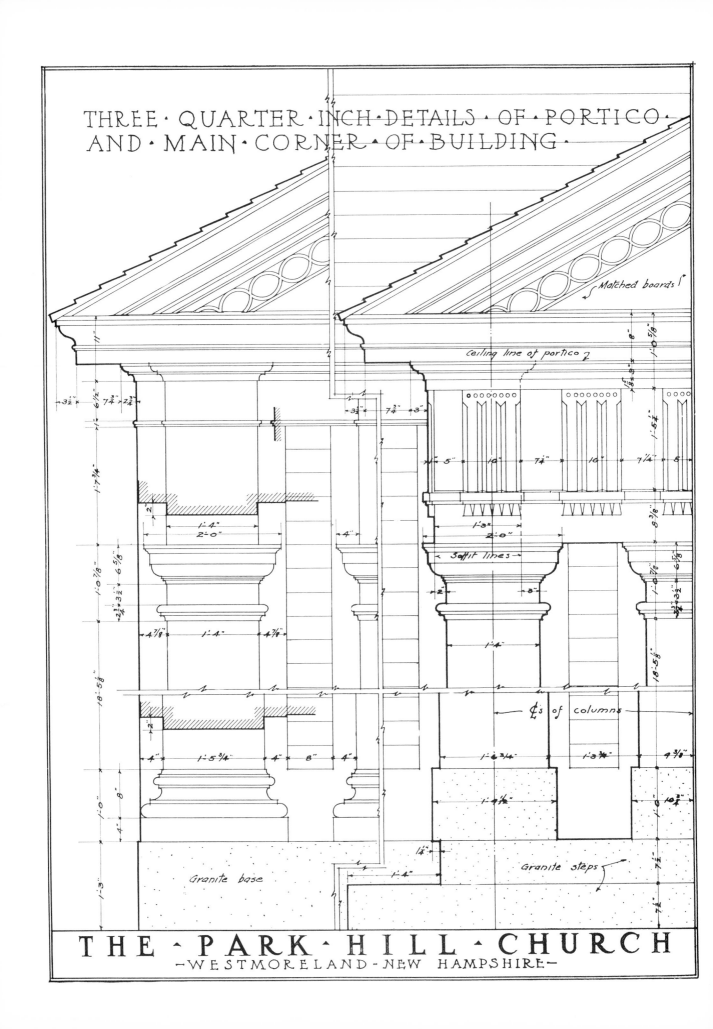

THREE · QUARTER · INCH · DETAILS · OF · PORTICO · AND · MAIN · CORNER · OF · BUILDING ·

Matched boards

Ceiling line of portico

Soffit lines

℄'s of columns

Granite base

Granite steps

THE · PARK · HILL · CHURCH
—WESTMORELAND· NEW · HAMPSHIRE—

PARK HILL CHURCH — 1824 — WESTMORELAND, NEW HAMPSHIRE

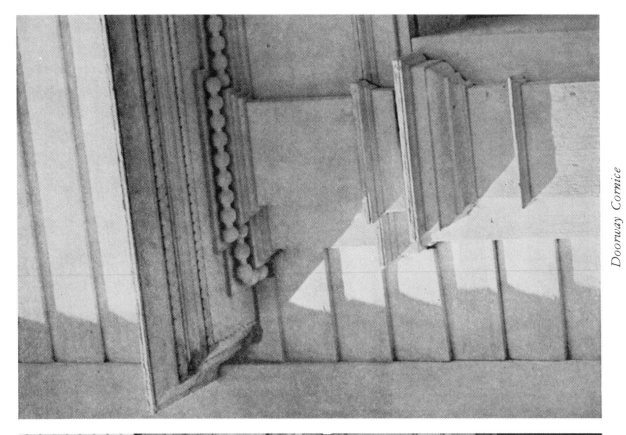

Doorway Cornice

Detail of Portico Cornice

PARK HILL CHURCH, WESTMORELAND, NEW HAMPSHIRE

CHURCH—1825—ACWORTH TOWN, NEW HAMPSHIRE

Doorway Detail

Detail of Entablature

CHURCH AT ACWORTH TOWN, NEW HAMPSHIRE

Detail of Spire
CHURCH AT ACWORTH TOWN, NEW HAMPSHIRE

Detail of Pediment
CHURCH AT ACWORTH TOWN, NEW HAMPSHIRE

Garrison Houses Along
the New England Frontier

Text by
Stuart Bartlett
Photographs by
Arthur C. Haskell
Originally published in 1933 as White Pine Monograph
Volume XIX, Number 3

NATHANIEL PEASLEE GARRISON HOUSE—1675–1680—WEST NEWBURY, MASSACHUSETTS

GARRISON HOUSES ALONG THE
NEW ENGLAND FRONTIER

THE "garrison house" of the Northern colonies was a distinct type developed to meet the needs of the various communities scattered along the border in the period of the King Philip and the several French and Indian wars. Except the brief unpleasantness, sometimes called the Pequot War, in 1637, and two short periods of Indian raiding in 1642 and 1653, most of the local Indian tribes remained on friendly terms with the settlers, until 1675, when King Philip's War broke out in June, in Plymouth County, Massachusetts. This was the first occasion for any general provision being made to protect the lives of the settlers from human enemies, and its real seriousness is indicated by the fact that during the fighting of 1675 through 1677 over six hundred colonists lost their lives, and an even larger number of homes were burned and destroyed; a very considerable drain upon the population and prosperity of the northern New England settlements at that time.

Following a dozen years of peace, another struggle began—often called King William's War—and continued from about 1688 or 1690 to 1697 or 1698. The Indians now came from farther afield, and were backed and instigated by the French in Canada. After a brief peace, from 1699 to 1703, Queen Anne's War broke out and waged until July of 1713, followed by another war with the French and Indians, known as Dummer's War, which lasted until the summer of 1726, when peace was signed at Falmouth (Portland) in the summer of that year and lasted for about

twenty years. These same hostilities are, farther north, sometimes known as Lovewell's War, and cost the colonies £170,000.

Deerfield, on the Connecticut River, is a well known example that shows, in the close clustering of its old houses along one short village street, the effect the Indian threat exerted upon its "community plan"! (See Volume VII, Chapter 6.)

Settled in 1669, the town street was laid out in 1671. Even as early as 1675, at the outbreak of the Indian wars, it had a little over a hundred inhabitants, with Hadley and Brookfield, its nearest neighbors, nearly fifty miles away. In 1688 the town was partially fortified, and the meeting house enclosed by a palisade. This palisade, or stockade, was a type of defense inherited from the Indians themselves and easily arranged in a country so naturally well wooded. Within this area could be gathered the livestock as well as the human beings of the surrounding community. The limits of the stockade could include some brook, spring or well; and often even a part of the garden food supply. Within this enclosed area it was also customary to provide a strong "blockhouse" or "garrison" to shelter better the men, women, and children—giving them space to cook, eat, and sleep under something approaching normal conditions, while a few rough "penthouses" might be provided to help protect the farm stock.

The garrison house ordinarily had two rooms to a floor and a chimney either in the center or at one or both ends. When the house was more than one story in height the upper walls might be of logs or plank. Sometimes the house had walls of only one story in height; sometimes there were two stories— in which case the upper always overhung the lower. The walls were built of heavy timber, cut to a usual seven inches thickness, ingeniously fitted together at the angles, and with musketry loopholes in the walls, and often one or two square "portholes" or shuttered openings about 12" by 16", or thereabouts, upon each front. The roofs seem to have been usually lightly built, with a heavily timbered floor in the attic which was always kept thoroughly covered with ashes or sand so that the lower part of the structure would be less apt to be ignited in case the Indians were able to set fire to the roof by means of their arrows.

Along the northern and western boundaries of the colonies the town records and histories are filled with references as to the methods taken to protect villages and homesteads, requiring all settlers to build only within limited distances of the garrison houses or churches (the first churches were often built as community houses of defense, as well!). A few fortunate communities already had—or were soon to construct—houses of brick which, because of their better resistance to fire, were at once utilized as "garrisons" or "houses of refuge" by those living nearby. Others arranged to have such houses built, or assisted in their construction, whenever possible, selecting locations upon raised hills or knolls conveniently central to some group of settlers or settlements.

An endeavor was made to have these "garrisons" occur at regular and fairly close

The Halliday Historic Photograph Co.

"OLD INDIAN HOUSE" GARRISON,
DEERFIELD, MASSACHUSETTS

intervals along the boundaries of the occupied and settled lands, or near important fords and river crossings. Meanwhile the more protected garrison houses continued to be occupied, with the window openings enlarged, the walls clapboarded outside for better protection against weather, and plastered for more modern convenience within, until it soon became difficult to trace their older purposes.

Structures of this characteristic type were built even in comparatively late years, and in protected communities. For instance, a "watch-house" was built in Ipswich, near the meeting house, as late as 1745; and two of the most interesting special buildings done for purposes of defense date from 1732 and 1738, and are still to be seen at Eliot, Maine; comparatively unchanged on the interior, though the exterior has been covered with clapboards and a large barn doorway cut through the closely matched logs of the larger in order to continue its usefulness and adapt it to the more profitable and peaceful pursuit of agriculture!

But these old "log garrisons" are the most indubitable and characteristic product of the problem and the times; the best examples of the architectural adaptation of local materials to a human need; the solution of the vital problem of providing "shelter"— in its most essential form—to the early inhabitants of the settlements in New England.

One of the oldest and most interesting of this group is the log garrison built at Exeter, N.H., by Councillor John Gilman probably between 1655 and 1657. He settled in Exeter and in 1647 with his brother Edward built and operated a saw mill at "the Falls," a few

Photo by W. S. Appleton, 1910

DAM-DREW-ROUNDS GARRISON,
DOVER, NEW HAMPSHIRE

hundred feet from the house. By 1657 he had sawn out and built nearby a two-story house of oak timber seven inches thick. The first story had the logs tenoned into upright corner posts which upheld a bracketed girt, overhanging the first story about ten inches. The floor was laid across the house, using logs about six inches thick and often two feet wide, set close together; and this puncheon floor construction is still to be seen in one room of the dwelling. The sec-

almost two feet below the older portion and raising the second-floor ceiling. At the same time he carried the new cornice and exterior treatment entirely around the structure, raising a new roof above the old and making the top row of glass lights in the new fifteen-light second-story windows above the top of the older window openings in the old "garrison" portion of the building! A part of the plaster wall in the northwest corner room of the old garrison, and also upon the

FROST FARM WITH GARRISON HOUSE AT REAR, EAST ELIOT, MAINE

ond story wall was built of timber of the same thickness, but the corners were dovetailed together. The story heights were low (about 6'-6"), and if the structure originally had a central chimney, it has now disappeared. A staircase has replaced the probable early steep ladder, and evidence has existed that indicates the entrance doorway was originally protected by a sliding grill or portcullis.

By about 1750 Councillor Peter Gilman had built on an ell across the west end to entertain John Wentworth, the last of the colonial governors, and increased the new story heights by lowering the first floor

newer stairway, has been removed so that the old timber wall of the early dwelling is exposed. The second-story room of the new ell is paneled on all four sides, although some of the rooms in the older portion contain paneled ends of earlier design and execution. In 1796, when Daniel Webster was fourteen years old and came to Exeter to study at the Academy, he lived in the rooms in the second floor, northwest corner, of the garrison part of the dwelling, which was then known as the Clifford house. Another garrison stood a short distance away on "the plains," the Janvrin Garrison, built in 1680 or earlier, but it has

Framing

Plank Stairs and Door

MAJOR CHARLES FROST GARRISON HOUSE—1738—EAST ELIOT, MAINE

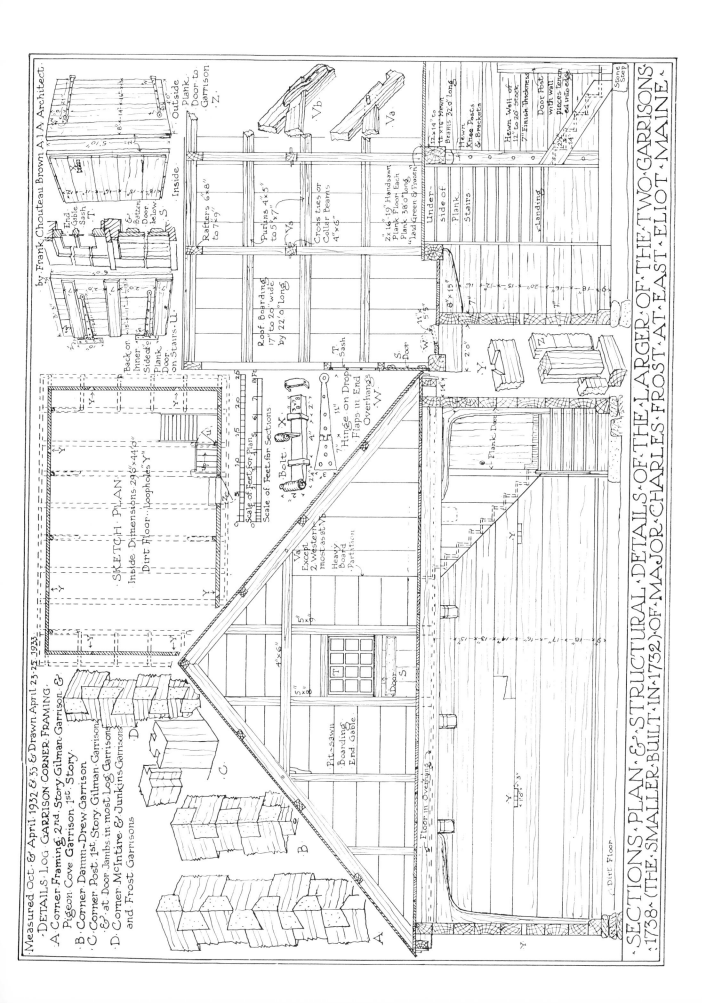

Measured Oct. & April 1932 & 3; & Drawn April 23-25, 1933.
by Frank Chouteau Brown A.I.A. Architect.

·DETAILS· LOG·GARRISON·CORNER·FRAMING·

·A· Corner·Framing· 2nd. Story·Gilman·Garrison· &
Pigeon·Cove·Garrison· 1st. Story.
·B· Corner· Damm~Drew·Garrison·
·C· Corner· Post· 1st. Story· Gilman·Garrison·
& at Door· Jambs in most Log·Garrisons·
·D· Corner· McIntire & Junkins·Garrisons·
and Frost Garrisons

·SKETCH·PLAN·
Inside·Dimensions 29'6"x44'9"
Dirt Floor~Loopholes "Y"

Scale of Feet for Plan.
Scale of Feet for Sections

·SECTIONS·PLAN· &· STRUCTURAL·DETAILS·OF·THE·LARGER·OF·THE·TWO·GARRISONS·
·1738· (THE·SMALLER·BUILT·IN·1732)·OF·MAJOR·CHARLES·FROST·AT·EAST·ELIOT·MAINE·

been so changed as to have lost all its old character. It had "planked walls."

In the Woodman Institute, at Dover, may still be seen the old Dam-Drew Garrison House, which was built by William Dam, son of Deacon John Dam, in 1675, in the "Back River" District in Dover Neck, about three miles south of Dover. It was removed to its present location in 1916. It is a one-story squared-log structure, 42' by 24'6" with a foot-wide overhang, carrying an 8" by 19" projecting plate against which the rafters rest. It was occupied continuously until

Photo by W. S. Appleton, 1911

BUNKER GARRISON HOUSE, DURHAM, N.H.

after the Civil War, when the weather began to get at the pins and corner notches (which were not cut on a slope to throw out the rain, as in most structures of this type). Hackmatack seems to have been the principal material from which the logs were squared. The chimney has been rebuilt —of smaller bricks than the original—but the interior partitions and arrangement have been retained, so that the visitor may here obtain as good an idea of the garrison log type as it is now possible to secure. Both the loopholes, and small openings about 10" by 12", are easily found.

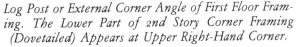

Log Post or External Corner Angle of First Floor Framing. The Lower Part of 2nd Story Corner Framing (Dovetailed) Appears at Upper Right-Hand Corner.

Inside of Exterior Corner, 2nd Floor Room. The Log in Which the Square Opening is Cut is About 21" High x 7" Thick. Sawn Log Faces Were Later Hacked to Hold Plaster.

GILMAN GARRISON HOUSE—1655–1657—EXETER, NEW HAMPSHIRE

Original Log Portion at Left. The 1750 Wing Shows Projected Beyond at Right.

Rear View of Original Log Garrison Portion

GILMAN GARRISON HOUSE — 1655–1657 — EXETER, NEW HAMPSHIRE

South (Fireplace) End

Peter Gilman Ell

GILMAN GARRISON HOUSE—1750—EXETER, NEW HAMPSHIRE

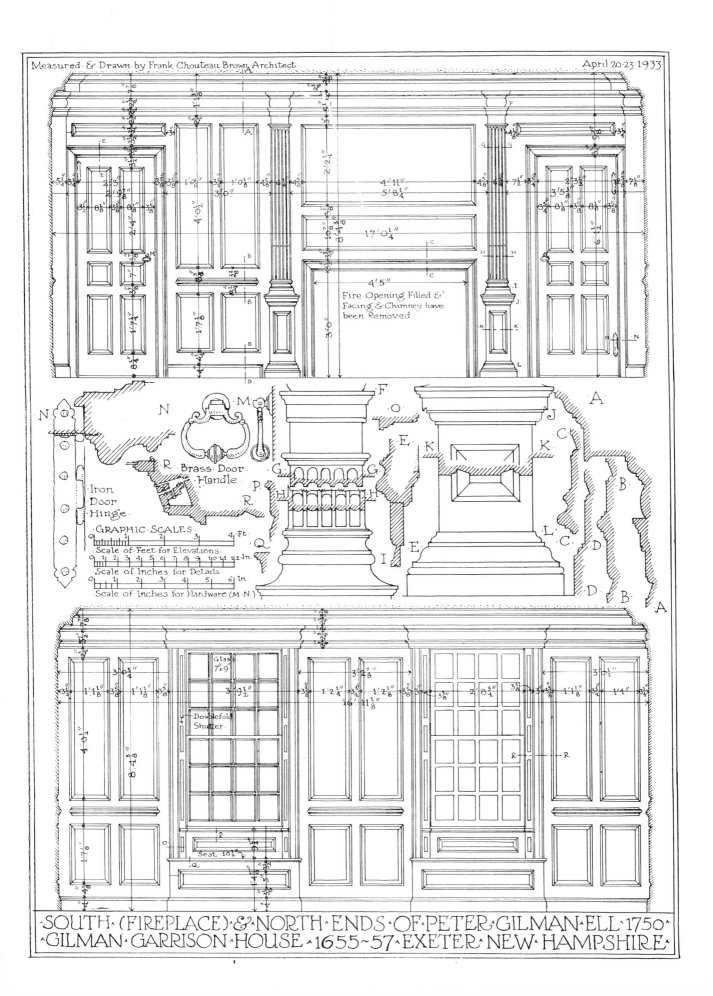

Measured & Drawn by Frank Chouteau Brown, Architect

April 20-23-1933

4'-11"
5'-8¼"

17'-0¼"

4'-5"

Fire Opening Filled &
Facing & Chimney have
been Removed

Iron
Door
Hinge

Brass Door
Handle

GRAPHIC SCALES

Scale of Feet for Elevations.

Scale of Inches for Details.

Scale of Inches for Hardware (M·N)

Glass
7"x 9"

Doublefold
Shutter

Seat 10½"

·SOUTH·(FIREPLACE)·&·NORTH·ENDS·OF·PETER·GILMAN·ELL·1750·
·GILMAN·GARRISON·HOUSE·1655~57·EXETER·NEW·HAMPSHIRE·

The Frost Garrisons, at East Eliot, Maine (pages 71–73), are the latest existing structures of the log type.

The large garrison was evidently intended to accommodate animals as well as human beings, and the perfection of the smooth hewn log surfaces, their close fit at the joints, both horizontal and end joinings, as well as the tightness of the pit-sawn plank floor, "laid green and frozen," are most remarkable today.

This section was especially open to Indian raids,

family. The corners were dovetailed, with sloping surfaces to throw out the water.

Another two-story garrison nearby, the Bunker Garrison (page 74), was measured as late as 1910. It was 40'-6" by 20'-9" outside, and the corner angles were notched, and the door posts had logs tenoned into them, while the top of the low doorway was cut into a slight segment of an arch in the under edge of the caplog.

McINTIRE GARRISON HOUSE—1640–1645—SCOTLAND, NEAR YORK, MAINE

and many garrisons were maintained here during the later years of the French and Indian wars. In 1695, twenty garrisons were listed in Durham as being maintained by the authorities, and each soldier cost the Province at the rate of £3 12s. 0d. board for eighteen weeks, according to the old records, while from one to four soldiers were quartered in each of the garrisons.

The only other easily recognizable garrison in southern Maine is the McIntire Garrison at Scotland (Brixham), on the Eliot side of York, which was built by Micum McIntire, and is still preserved by that

There are many old brick garrisons in this northern section, some of which were originally built with that purpose in mind, and others adapted to it as being the "most defensible" in their locality.

Thomas Duston, who had settled in Kittery in 1654, afterwards removed to the top of a hill outside Haverhill—then Pentucket—where he experimented in making bricks, finally building the present house of them some time during 1696–1697, with "floors and roof of white oak."

Haverhill, Massachusetts, occupied an important

point on what remained the northern frontier of the New England colonies for nearly seventy years. The town records of 1690 show the appointment of six garrison houses, and four "houses of refuge."

In describing the characteristics of the houses located in that vicinity, Mirick writes: "Most of the garrisons and two of the houses of refuge—those belonging to Joseph and Nathaniel Peaslee—were built of brick, and were two stories high; those that were not built of this

entered the chamber with the help of a ladder instead of stairs so that the inmates could retreat into them and take it up if the basement-story should be taken by the enemy. Their fireplaces were of such enormous sizes that they could burn their wood, sled-length, very conveniently, and the ovens opened on the outside of the building, generally at one end."

This description well applies to the Hazzen-Spiller House, a listed garrison, built in 1724, about three-

DICKENSON-PILLSBURY-WITHAM HOUSE—1700—GEORGETOWN, MASSACHUSETTS

material had a single laying of it between the outer and the inner walls. They had but one outside door, which was often so small that but one person could enter at a time; their windows were about two feet and a half in length, eighteen inches in breadth, and were secured on the inside with iron bars. Their glass was very small, cut in the shape of a diamond, was extremely thick, and fastened in with lead instead of putty. There were generally but two rooms in the basement (first) story, and tradition says that they

quarters of a mile below the center of the town.

The Dickenson-Pillsbury-Witham House, built on a knoll beside the road in Georgetown, near the Rowley line, previous to 1700, is described in an early family record, as follows: "It was built in the time of the Indian depredations. My great-grandmother occupied it in the time of the Indians. It was lined from the sill to the girth with bricks between the plastering and the boards. There were doors outside the windows to shut at night. The outside doors were barred inside. One night the Indians came and attacked the house, making an attempt to cut the outside (doors) down to get into the house. My great-grandmother took a pail of scalding water, went upstairs, and poured it onto their heads, and they were glad to retire." J. L. Ewell, in his *Story of Byfield, a New England Parish,* further adds: "In these houses, the second story frequently projected over the lower one for defense against the Indian, and the roof ran down

a beautifully carved wooden latch on the great cellar door, a crane five or six feet attached to a great beam in the ceiling to swing out and hold candlesticks suspended by trammels and wooden partitions dressed of old with blue clay and skim milk in lieu of paint." This original surfacing can still be seen on portions of the woodwork in this room shown below.

Paul Pillsbury, one of its inhabitants, in the war of 1812, shouldered and carried a cannon weighing seven

DICKENSON-PILLSBURY-WITHAM GARRISON HOUSE—1700—GEORGETOWN, MASSACHUSETTS

to the lower story in the rear, making a back 'linter' (lean-to). In the huge chimney was the bench where the family could sit cozily and watch the great fire of logs or read by its light. Mr. Witham's house is probably an heirloom from the seventeenth century. Its architecture closely resembles that of the old house on Kent's Island, not now standing, that was said to have been built in 1653. The large living room has a huge fireplace in which two cook-stoves stand side by side,

hundred pounds. He invented in this house the "peg machine" that revolutionized the shoe business in New England, selling pegs for eight cents a quart or $2.00 a bushel—that formerly had to be painfully split and whittled by hand out of maple by the shoe makers. The first cut nails were also made nearby, in a factory on the Parker River, where were also the first cotton and woolen mills in America, dating from 1636, and the first fulling mill, from 1643.

HAZZEN-SPILLER GARRISON HOUSE — 1724 — HAVERHILL, MASSACHUSETTS
Building restored in 1917.

JOSEPH PEASLEE GARRISON—1675—ROCK VILLAGE, MASS.

DUSTON GARRISON HOUSE—1696-1697—HAVERHILL, MASS.
Only one of the old windows remains in the attic of the front gable.

The Boston Post Road

With Text by

Text by
Peter Augustus Pindar
Photographs by
Kenneth Clark
Originally published in 1920 as White Pine Monograph
Volume VI, Number 1

HOUSE AT GUILFORD, CONNECTICUT

THE BOSTON POST ROAD

THE earliest settlement in Connecticut was made not along the shore, but in its center at Hartford. This is rather curious, since the history of all colonization has been that settlements in new countries have been made first at the ports, and have then expanded up the navigable rivers. One would have expected, then, that the first settlements in Connecticut would have been made in some of its many excellent harbors, at New London perhaps, or New Haven or Bridgeport, and that colonization would have spread first up the Naugatuck, the Connecticut and Thames rivers, and along the shore of the Sound.

But the settlement was made by men from Massachusetts who advanced overland, and, finding fertile bottom land and a smiling soft countryside along the Connecticut River, founded a little group of colonies around Hartford and Wethersfield. The Connecticut shore was colonized not long after, and as trade developed each little coastal town became the metropolis of the farming community in the neighboring back country.

As means of transportation improved, various cities attained positions of dominance, and instead of a dozen or so small metropolises on the northern coast of the United States, Boston and New York became of great importance, while the other cities dropped into subordinate positions, and either grew very slowly, as was the case with New Haven and New London for many years, or actually receded in population, as, for example, Stonington and Essex. These smaller towns became little more than halting places on the famous old Boston Post Road from New York to Boston, but their inhabitants had already laid the solid foundations of small fortunes, and settling down to a quiet, unhurried life, built for themselves in the closing years of the eighteenth century groups of homes which were in their day of an average quality and cost as high as in any other part of the colonies. Further, since most of the towns have grown hardly at all, and are for the most part beyond the zone of commutation travel to New York or Boston, the houses which served the people a hundred and thirty or forty years ago, have been adequate for their descendants. Where in the big and prosperous cities the proportion of old houses is almost negligible, and the absolute number very few, in the small old towns one could almost fancy one was miraculously returned to the Colonial period, so many old wood-built houses remain.

The settlement was of course by English people, and because the character of the country has changed so little, the names of the towns themselves are a pleasure to hear, recalling visions of old times. The terminology is singularly free from "made-up" names which sound like the titles of a train of Pullman cars; they are all simple English town names, used in tender recollection of the birthplaces of their founders, with one or two reminiscences of Indian nomenclature; and to call them over is to bring to mind the pleasant land of Kent and Sussex and Surrey from which their early settlers came: Westport, Bridgeport, Fairfield, New Haven, Branford, Guilford, Clinton, Saybrook, Lyme and New London — old towns for us, older towns in England.

They are singularly alike even today, and must once have been so closely similar that the colonial traveler who took the Boston stage-coach from New York to his home town must have been uncertain as to when he arrived, unless he had ticked off the places as he passed. They were as alike as beads on the string of the Boston Post Road—beads of the same pattern and the same color. Each little town centered around the "green," usually a rectangle nearly square, but sometimes an irregular central space between converging roads, perhaps a long narrow rectangle, or a triangle. Each green was dominated by the church, and the churches, even, were so alike that they offered no convenient means of identification: they were, in fact, often copied directly from others in neighboring towns, as when the trustees of Lyme contracted to have built "a fair copy" of the North Church in New Haven. The stores were hardly distinguishable from the houses, and indeed most shops were only parts of houses devoted to selling things; show windows were uncommon, and those which existed were divided into small panes because it was not yet known how to make large sheets of glass.

The houses, too, were very much alike, simple square boxes, usually two stories in height, with fairly low pitched gable roofs. Occasionally one-story houses with rather steeper roofs were built, and sometimes gambrel roofs were employed on both one and two story houses. The plans showed a little variety, being almost always contained in a nearly square rectangle, so that the mass was a simple block, sometimes relieved by low wings, although these were usually later additions. Even piazzas or covered porches did not form part of the original design, so that these old houses depended for their beauty upon two things only: the proportion of a very simple

mass, and the excellence of the sparingly employed detail in cornices, doorways and windows. Pilasters or engaged columns were sometimes used to decorate the principal façades, and sometimes there was a change of material in the first story from that in the balance of the house, but usually the wall surfaces were of clapboards spaced with apparent regularity.

With such simple motives, it is astonishing that the designers could obtain any variety in appearance, and that they were able to make the houses so uniformly lovely. Most modern architects would be put to it were they compelled to work within such narrow limits and with so few opportunities to introduce new motives; yet the old carpenter-architects appeared to be able to produce endless variations of a very simple theme, each worthy of study. Apparently their greatest question was as to whether the front or the gable end should be placed to the street; when the gable end was the main façade they often ornamented it to a degree with them unusual.

Once in a while we find a house which has a plan different from the standard one to a marked degree, and in these the designers evidently felt very strongly the need for symmetry. Take, for example, the Jessup House at Westport; this house has a gable in the center flanked by short wings with hip roofs. Curiously enough neither of the two doorways is in the gable end but they flank it in the wings; and they are by no means as much ornamented as is customary in doorways of this period, but are rather suppressed to accentuate the importance of the central gable end. The extreme slenderness of the engaged columns expresses their purely decorative purpose, and the arches over the windows and the panels below them illustrate very well the way in which

Window Detail
JESSUP HOUSE, WESTPORT, CONNECTICUT

JESSUP HOUSE, WESTPORT, CONNECTICUT

OLD ACADEMY, FAIRFIELD, CONNECTICUT

the later colonial designers used plain surfaces of flush boards as a decoration.

One of the most interesting of the buildings along the Post Road is the old Academy, now used as a tea-room, in Fairfield. It was built, as its name indicates, for a boys' school; and its designer evidently felt that its semipublic purpose should be expressed on its façade. This he did by introducing a pediment over the five center bays, and projecting the wall below five or six inches from the main wall. The cupola or

through an unbroken succession of little towns which, at least in their central features, have changed little in the last hundred years. We can still form an excellent idea of how Branford, Guilford, Clinton, Saybrook, Lyme and Mystic appeared from the top of the mail stage; or, indeed, from any one of the towns we could know how the others must have looked. Most of them still have at least one old church with four tall columns down the front and an excellent classic tower over the main entrance; the old greens are

HOUSE AT GROTON CENTER, CONNECTICUT

lantern is in its present state new, but replaces a former one. The charm of the building is largely in the plain end walls and the flush boards used in the gables and pediment; the detail is not very interesting, but the three doorways, the pediment and the cupola make a quaintly dignified little public building.

New Haven has grown to be a pretty big city itself, but still retains some relics of the time when it was still a toy colonial city. The old churches still dominate the green, and around it are two or three of the old houses, of type similar to those in the little towns along the Post Road. Going east from New Haven along the road all the way to New London, we pass

well kept and filled with old elms, and surrounded by square white houses appearing to regard the green, over the white picket fences which surround them, with an air demurely discreet. Of these houses the several varieties are illustrated: the beautifully placed square old house at Guilford, with its tiny dooryard, shows in its roof of unequal pitches a reminiscence of the seventeenth-century work; the house on the Post Road near Saybrook is as nearly typical of the locality and the period as it is possible to imagine; one of the "early settlers" survives in Groton Center, bearing a tablet which states that "Whitefield the Evangelist preached from a platform erected level with the upper windows

HOUSE AT OLD MYSTIC, CONNECTICUT

OLD ACADEMY, FAIRFIELD, CONNECTICUT

HOUSE NEAR WESTBROOK, CONNECTICUT

HOUSE AT GROTON CENTER, CONNECTICUT

STAUNTON HOUSE, CLINTON, CONNECTICUT

HOUSE AT OLD LYME, CONNECTICUT

Doorway

HOUSE AT GROTON CENTER,
CONNECTICUT

of this house, June, 1764." Curious inscription! It interests us because of its very humanity, the quality it has of small town gossip. Very likely, not one out of fifty who reads it with edification has the remotest idea of who was "Whitefield the Evangelist," or even a very clear idea as to what an evangelist is or was. The inscription fails to inform us where the platform was erected. Was it against this house, or across the road, or in some neighboring state? And why should this house have been used as a standard of measurement? Yet it is a curiously satisfactory inscription, and one leaves with real pleasure at knowing that the platform was so high, and hopes that the preacher didn't fall off.

Some of the houses are of the humbler sort — farmers' or fishermen's cottages; but all alike are pervaded by the same peaceful spirit which holds the whole countryside in a sort of spell. It must be a very happy life to be a fisherman in the town with the most enthralling name in America — Mystic; though Qu'appelle in Quebec Province also has its claim. Mystic has not grown at all, but sits on its Mystic River, dreaming of the days when its whale-ships brought back souvenirs from Tahiti and the Marquesas. New London, on the other hand, has grown great, or at least greater than it was,

and is fortunate in having one of the few public buildings of colonial days extant — the county court house — from which we gain a very clear conception of what was our ancestors' idea of grandeur. We have advanced beyond them in the understanding of what size is, and what art is, but we can still learn from the quiet dignity of this beautiful old building the value of pure design.

Our ancestors' conception of what was requisite to elevate a building to the dignity of a court house differed from ours, less in the choice of motives than in their size. Pilasters today are the things we most commonly use to impress upon the beholder the fact that the building they adorn is one of importance, but where we would indicate the size of the rooms by running the pilasters the full height of the building, the older designers prefer to superimpose their orders. There are few or no elements we can select from the design of this building which identify it as a public building rather than a residence, and yet its motives subtly express its purpose. The material of which it is composed, the scale of the detail, the general mass and even the lantern are not in any sense distinct from the same motives in private house work; the pathetic attempts

Doorway

HOUSE AT OLD LYME, CONNECTICUT

to produce a sense of solidity by the introduction of quoins on the first story and heavy key blocks over the windows are not distinguishing features of this building, or even of other old public buildings.

The same characteristics mark most of the early American public buildings, as for example the New York City Hall and Independence Hall in Philadelphia; the purpose was rarely expressed by magnifying the size of motives, but rather by their multiplication, and it would seem with real benefit to the dignity and quality of their work. A large row of columns is unquestionably an impressive feature, but there seems to be a limit to the size to which they can profitably be used; to increase them beyond this limit is rather an evidence of paucity of imagination than of a lofty conception. It will be remembered that Guy Lowell won the competition for the New York County Court House with a design which was least in scale of all those submitted, and the enormous columns which were the dominating feature of many of the designs submitted became ludicrous when the true scale of the exterior was indicated by Mr. Lowell's drawings. It must also be remembered that there is no problem in classic architecture more difficult than to super-

Doorway

HOUSE AT OLD MYSTIC, CONNECTICUT

impose orders, especially more than two in number, yet it is a problem which the early architects solved in general much better than we. The greatest difficulty is probably to combine the cornice of the building with the entablature of the uppermost order; certain of our architects have even tried to decorate skyscrapers from top to bottom with applied orders of two or three stories each; it is obvious that it is impossible to reconcile the scale of the cornice of a thirty-foot order with that of a three-hundred-foot building. In this little court house at New London, the two-story building is perfectly terminated with a cornice of excellent scale as regards the order of which it is an integral part.

It is impossible to say just why we are so rarely able to approximate the quality of colonial work. Certainly we are better educated in architecture—or should we say *more* educated? We have a wider field of precedent from which to draw and we have more money and better mechanics with the same quality white pine as a building material, yet the colonial architect showed within his limited field a more daring talent for design, and a greater perfection in execution.

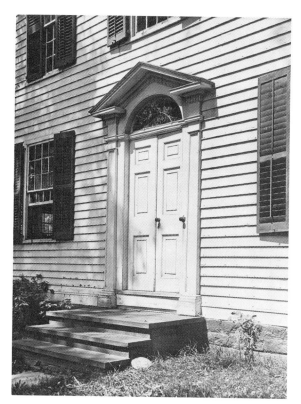

Doorway

HOUSE NEAR SAYBROOK, CONNECTICUT

COUNTY COURT HOUSE, NEW LONDON, CONNECTICUT

Stagecoach Road From
Hartford to Litchfield

Text by
Peter Augustus Pindar
Photographs by
The Author

Originally published in 1923 as White Pine Monograph
Volume IX, Number 5

SHELDON TAVERN, LITCHFIELD, CONNECTICUT

Built in 1760 by Elisha Sheldon for a residence but used as an inn by his son Samuel until 1780.
Also known as the Gould House until 1871.

THE STAGECOACH ROAD
FROM HARTFORD TO LITCHFIELD

HARTFORD was the first settlement in Connecticut, an outpost of the Massachusetts colony planted to keep off the Dutch of New Amsterdam who claimed the fertile valley of the Connecticut River for their own. Established in 1636 at a most excellent point near the head of navigation on the river, and in the center of the most fertile part of the state, Hartford early became a little metropolis, from which roads were thrown out to the farming country around it; and as the early settlements grew and became in themselves little centers, stagecoach lines were established to accommodate the growing travel.

Of these subordinate centers Litchfield was one, although just why the town should have had even local importance, is hard to say. The site of Litchfield is a lovely one, but it is on top of a rather high and steep hill, and the surrounding country is so rough and broken that it could never have been a very productive farming region. Nor were there other industries which could cause growth; there were excellent deposits of iron ore some twenty miles away, and splendid water power at Falls Village on the Housatonic River, near the Massachusetts state line, but though these were discovered and used early in the eighteenth century, neither Salisbury nor Falls Village have ever grown very much, while Litchfield was not only a town large by colonial standards but a very wealthy little place.

So of the early stage lines, out of Hartford, one ran to Litchfield over the level valley to Farmington, a beautiful old town settled in 1640. The road crosses the Farmington River and continues up the fertile river valley to Unionville, where the road

Litchfield Stagecoach under Shed
OLD TAVERN (NOW COLONIAL MUSEUM), DANBURY

crossed the river again, and ascended a steep ravine to Burlington. Then came a long stretch of road along the bottom of a narrow rough valley to Harwinton and East Litchfield, where the Naugatuck River was crossed, and the four mile steep climb to Litchfield was begun.

The exact date at which this line was established is not known, but it was certainly before 1755, and the line still ran in 1870, when the railroad killed horse-drawn competition, and the old stages were

Most of the old stagecoach roads, or post roads — they were both — have long since been improved beyond recognition, for generally speaking, the towns of importance a century ago are the towns of importance today; but this old road from Litchfield as far as Unionville remains as it was, and were it possible, some old gentleman who left the Phelps Tavern in Litchfield at six o'clock in the morning, Standard Time (it is a misdemeanor to use Daylight Saving Time in Connecticut) on August 19,

JOHNSON HOUSE—1690—FARMINGTON, CONNECTICUT

sold off. They must have built these stages well, for tradition says that some of them were sent to Deadwood, Montana, and that the Deadwood coach which Buffalo Bill used to dramatize was one of them, brought across the continent. Nor was this the only hard usage they withstood, for until the trolley ran to Farmington, the girls of Miss Porter's School were met in Hartford by one of them. This particular coach is still extant and was under a shed of the late Mr. Ives' Colonial Museum at Danbury, as recently as September of this year, when it was to be sold at auction.

1823 he would have found few changes had he traveled with Mr. Whitehead and myself on the same day in 1923. Even the road cannot have been much improved, although he might have been somewhat surprised at the new fangled vehicle (our automobile) in which he found himself traveling.

He would have regretted to find at the bottom of the steep hill on East Street a half mile from the tavern, where we cross the brook, that the old mill has been burned down and has not been rebuilt, but he should have been pleased to see that the oldest house in Litchfield was being restored.

Doorway and Overhang

WHITMAN HOUSE, FARMINGTON CONNECTICUT

Overhang embellished by drop ornament

RICHARDS HOUSE, LITCHFIELD, CONNECTICUT
Built about 1730. Restorations soon to be made.

I doubt if he would have known how old it was, for it was standing in his great-grandfather's time, and his great-great-grandfather died in 1730. He would have probably been glad that if the old door didn't suit, and Mis' Richards had to hire one of these new-fangled architects to make her a new one, that she picked on young Mr. Woolsey, one of the old Yale family, you know. But the new door is so in keeping with the old house that he probably wouldn't have noticed the change.

Across the road he would have recognized Echo Farm with its tiny porch and Palladian window and would have felt no comment necessary; it looks just the same as it always did; and from Echo Farm to East Litchfield he would have found only one new house, although in the small plain farmsteads along the road he would have found Zuccas and Bodanskis working the fields which used to belong to Demmings and Fosters.

He might have wondered at the new concrete bridge and the railroad tracks at East Litchfield had we let him see them, but by our agreeable conversation, we would have diverted his mind until we had crossed the new state road up the Naugatuck Valley, and had turned up what looks like the yard of the corner farmhouse into the road to Harwinton; and as we climbed the long mile to the tavern at the cross road to Torrington, he would have seen no change at all, for there is no house or relic of a house in that mile.

He (having come from 1823) would have wanted to stop for a little refreshment at the tavern, but it has long since been closed, and is now very rusty and down at heel; and then we would have driven another two miles along a narrow tree shaded soggy road until we came to what was in his day the newest house in Harwinton, the Wilson House on which the paint had but dried in 1833. The man who built the Wilson House wasn't any of your backwoods builders! He knew a thing or two about this new Greek architecture Asher Benjamin had written a book about, and he got some of the best of it into this house, even if Mr. Wilson did insist on the recessed side porch so fashionable in Har-

ECHO FARM — c1737 — LITCHFIELD, CONNECTICUT

winton but on this porch he used what was called the "column in antis" motive with two story columns two feet in diameter. These so obstructed the porch that an irreverent generation has taken them out and stored them in the barn.

Harwinton would have seemed very familiar to our passenger, for while he would have noticed some "new" houses built around 1830 (in the biggest and best of which Henry Hornbostel lives) he would have been glad to see the old Academy behind the Messenger House, and would probably have regretted as we did that the cupola has been taken off and a tin roof substituted for the ancient shingles. But the Messenger House, once the home of the family of the first settlers in Harwinton, is in perfect condition, probably because it is owned by a gentleman who lives in what our passenger knew as Fort Duquesne.

The old fellow would have told us some interesting things about Harwinton; how it was settled in 1686 partly by people from Hartford, and partly by people from Windsor; and how those two towns

quarreled so over the new settlement that it finally set up for itself on the 11th of May in 1733, choosing as its name the combination Haw-win-ton from Hart-ford-town, and Wind-sor-town. But he could have told us what his father had very likely *not* told him, of how many hogsheads of cider and barrels of rum were drunk when they "raised" the church.

If he had been told what we were doing he would have been sorry not to see us stop and photograph the church which is one of the most delightful of the old New England meeting houses with a steeple, in what Mr. Hornbostel called the Chippendale style, which may be that too, for all I know, although it is almost a literal copy of another church on the Litchfield-Hartford road, the one at Farmington. The old Town Hall, which must have been new in his day has unfortunately been destroyed and replaced by a brick building which Mr. Hornbostel, the architect, has thoughtfully designed following the motive of the old one and set upon the original stone foundation.

But if he had inquired at any of the houses after

Doorway Detail
BROWN INN, BURLINGTON, CONNECTICUT

Doorway Detail
RICHARDS HOUSE, LITCHFIELD, CONNECTICUT

Doorway

MESSENGER HOUSE—1783—HARWINTON, CONNECTICUT

Doorway

HOUSE—1780—HARWINTON, CONNECTICUT

WILSON HOUSE — 1833 — HARWINTON, CONNECTICUT

OLD HARWINTON ACADEMY — 1783 — HARWINTON, CONNECTICUT

the families of his old friends, and found them gone, he would probably not have been much surprised, for in 1820 there were only five families among the seventeen hundred and eighteen inhabitants, who had lived for twenty years in their original houses. These Harwinton people always were a restless lot.

By that time the old fellow would have been thirsty, missing his morning toddy at the Torring-day the luncheon stop of the stages. In this plain little building five generations of Abijah Catlins kept tavern, and among the guests included General Washington and General Lafayette as well as many of the ancient Litchfield worthies. The stage route must have been much frequented, and the inn popular, for the second or third Abijah built himself a big comfortable house across the road from the inn, and spared no expense to make it

MESSENGER HOUSE — 1783 — HARWINTON, CONNECTICUT

ton Corner Inn, and without letting us stop at the Birge House or the Stone House, (so called because the lintels and sills are of stone, although the house itself was of brick with a wooden cornice and an entrancing old elliptical headed fanlight and sidelight on the doorway) he would have hurried us up the hill to the old inn built in 1745 by one of the Abijah Catlins, and which was in my friend's the finest house in Harwinton, finer even than the Messenger House in the green. But our passenger has joined us a little too late, for only last year the last of Catlins sold the house to some foreigners from Torrington! The Catlin Homestead now owned by the Clevelands is really about as representative a piece of Connecticut architecture as one could wish for. It has all the motives which are distinctly of Connecticut origin, including a delightful Palladian window above the door and sidelights like those in the Kingsberry House at Litchfield and the Cowles House at Farmington, although the treatment of them is flatter, the pilasters taking the place of columns in the lower border and even the balustrades being sawn boards instead of turned. The side porch has the two story free standing order within a recess, of which the examples in

it to its original condition both in design and furnishings, a thing which we do not always have the luck to find.

The five miles from Harwinton to Burlington would have shown our passenger nothing either old or new except a couple of pleasant old farmhouses, built about the time of his last trip; and we would have set him down in Burlington at the Brown Inn, facing the green with its small pa-

HOUSE — c1810 — HARWINTON CONNECTICUT

Woodbury and Litchfield have been already illustrated in this series and in the gable ends in the third story sort of baby Palladian window lights the attic. The house is unfortunately on the south side of the road and shadowed by very heavy trees so that a successful photograph of it is almost impossible. It really is one of the most notable houses in New England and its pleasant owners appreciate this fact and are proposing to restore

thetic monument to the town's dead in the World War. Around the green he would have seen old friends, and no intruders; but he would have sighed to see them so forlorn, the lovely porch of the inn shorn of its columns, and the houses grimy and unkempt except for one smart little house at the head of the green where the road to Winsted forks from the old stagecoach road. And there in that little forgotten town we will leave him; for Bur-

ABIJAH CATLIN HOMESTEAD—1795—HARWINTON, CONNECTICUT
It has all the motives which are distinctly of Connecticut origin.

ABIJAH CATLIN HOUSE—1795—HARWINTON, CONNECTICUT

POST ROAD INN, HARWINTON, CONNECTICUT
Built by one of the Abijah Catlins in 1745.

HOUSE AT THE HEAD OF THE GREEN, BURLINGTON, CONNECTICUT

lington was once great enough to be included in English atlases which did not show busy Torrington or Winsted. It has not grown but fallen into decay; while were we to take the old gentleman to Unionville his heart would break; it is full of knitting mills; and, dead as it is we like Burlington best.

CONGREGATIONAL CHURCH, FARMINGTON, CONNECTICUT
The church at Harwinton is almost a literal copy of this one.

College and Educational
Buildings in
New England

Text by
Eldon L. Dean
Photographs by
Arthur C. Haskell
Originally published in 1934 as White Pine Monograph
Volume XX, Number 6

PEARSON HALL—1817—PHILLIPS ANDOVER ACADEMY, ANDOVER, MASSACHUSETTS

Charles Bulfinch, Architect

EARLY COLLEGE AND EDUCATIONAL
BUILDINGS IN NEW ENGLAND

IN many instances the original structures associated with the beginnings of early educational institutions in New England have long disappeared; or been superseded by later buildings, themselves already of considerable age and association. It was also the fact that in many cases the buildings first used for educational purposes were not especially constructed for that use; but merely adapted to the purpose. Classes for the younger children in the early colonies, in many locations in New England, usually known as Dame Schools, were carried on in the homes of the "Dame" in whose charge the instruction of the children had been placed; or sometimes in another house more conveniently located, or of larger size, and therefore selected for the gathering of these small groups of local pupils of many varying ages.

No example of a small village schoolhouse, of an early date, especially built for the education of the younger scholars, is known still to exist in northern New England. A considerable number of one-room schoolhouse buildings may yet be found, scattered over some sections of Massachusetts, Rhode Island, Connecticut, Vermont, New Hampshire, and Maine—but usually they do not date from before 1830 to 1840. Some few have been kept nearly in their original condition (having been superseded by newer and larger buildings, and the "bus" system now in general use in rural communities having made them of no use on their original sites) but have been long closed and allowed to exist without care or repair. Many have

disappeared, from fire or neglect, but a few still "carry on," remote and forlorn. Many more have been changed or adapted to other uses; perhaps to serve as a "Union Church"; made into a farm cottage; occasionally they have become studios for some summer artist; or have fallen to the use of a roadside stand or gas filling station!

One or two examples of these simple structures, that may be regarded as more or less representative of the "little old red schoolhouse" of storied tradition (although, as a matter of fact, about as often "white" as "red" in the locality here represented!) are illustrated in this number; one—now actually a summer studio—conveniently located adjacent to the dismantled remains of an old "town pump" was the first public schoolhouse of Rockport, Massachusetts!

New England early town records carry many stories of the old "academies" that were founded in most towns of any importance; some of which languished for many years before the rising ascendency and success of the larger college institutions caused them to be abandoned. But a few have survived; some even flourishing today as accommodations for the younger scholars, in those localities where constant growth of surrounding towns and villages have made the need of an intermediate institution of this sort of continued neighborhood value. And two or three typical buildings illustrate this group of institutional architecture; the most pretentious being the three-story Derby Academy, in the old town of Hingham, in Massachu-

FIRST PUBLIC SCHOOLHOUSE, ROCKPORT, MASS.

SCHOOL AT GLOUCESTER, MASSACHUSETTS

setts, representative of the later and more prosperous structures of the period when these academies most flourished; another being the original building (1763) of the little academy founded and named after Lieut.-

Governor Dummer in Byfield, Massachusetts. Both these institutions are still flourishing and maintain a long record of educational ideals; although both now serve a far larger area than was ever contemplated as

DUMMER ACADEMY — ORIGINAL BUILDING 1763 — BYFIELD, MASSACHUSETTS

possible at the time of their foundation.

Of the old college buildings in this section, it must at once be acknowledged that the earliest buildings of the first institutions founded for the inculcation of learning have long since disappeared! There is every probability that those first constructed entirely for this

the Society for the Preservation of New England Antiquities for April, 1933, Vol. XXIII, No. 4; illustrated by some drawings of conjectural restorations of the first building at Harvard College, in Cambridge, made by Perry, Shaw & Hepburn, the "Old College," which was built in 1638 and finally destroyed in 1679.

DERBY ACADEMY, HINGHAM, MASSACHUSETTS

purpose must have followed examples established by earlier collegiate buildings of European precedent, particularly in England. Those especially interested in these earliest structures may be referred to the article by Professor Samuel E. Morison in the publication of

It was modeled upon the sort of Tudor structure that may still be seen in some of the earlier colleges in Cambridge, England.

But actually none of the earliest existing collegiate structures to be found in New England exhibits any architectural Tudor characteristics—unless perhaps what are claimed as remainders of the old single "studies" of the English colleges—small rooms about 5'0" x 8'0"—some of which are still to be seen in the present Hollis Hall, in Harvard (though now used as lavatories or closets), may be considered as such a survival!

As a matter of fact, Harvard University preserves more early buildings than are to be found in any other college among the northern New England states; in their original exterior aspect, at least. It is acknowledged that the changes caused by accident, fire, wear, and usage have left little of their interior finish or structure in original condition. Among its earlier buildings are Massachusetts Hall, 1720; Hollis Hall, 1763; Harvard Hall, 1766; Stoughton Hall, 1805; Holworthy Hall, 1812; and Holden Chapel, 1744. All these are built of brick, and are representative of their periods, only Harvard Hall having been very much altered upon its exterior by later changes and additions. The yard also boasts of University Hall, the fine granite structure designed by Charles Bulfinch.

Brown University in Providence has preserved three of its first structures, University Hall, 1773; Hope College, 1825; and Manning Hall, the latter a fine example of the Greek Revival influence, dating from 1833. Some of the other smaller colleges have also kept one or two of their earlier buildings, though generally of later date than those listed.

Both at Cambridge and Providence, the buildings dating from before the Revolution were used during the war as barracks for soldiers; and at Harvard, both Massachusetts and Hollis have been largely rebuilt inside, having been used both for recitation rooms and dormitories at different times. Fires have also damaged the interiors of parts of these buildings, causing new firewalls to be installed, and many minor changes in stairways and interior partitions have had to be made from time to time.

These same factors have even extended to affect most of the structures dating from early in the nineteenth century; and have in some cases even altered their exterior appearance; as has been the case with several of the older buildings at Phillips Andover

ABBOTT HALL—1829—ABBOTT ACADEMY, ANDOVER, MASSACHUSETTS

FRAMINGHAM ACADEMY, FRAMINGHAM, MASSACHUSETTS

Academy, for instance. Here no less than four of the existing buildings were designed by Bulfinch; but it is obvious, from any close study of the structures themselves, that their present state exhibits evidence that many changes—sometimes of considerable importance —have been made at various times to affect their fabric and exterior appearance. In the case of these particular structures, for instance, the belfries or cupolas are obviously not in their original relation to the designs. A large part of Pearson Hall, on both principal façades, show considerable areas of brickwork of a different period from the rest of the building; and several of the entrances exhibit evidences of changes and alterations that may have extensively varied their exterior appearance.

In general, however, despite changes in openings and roof lines; the additions of dormers, roof balustrades, or cupolas; these early college buildings are among the most interesting records of early brick masonry that have been preserved from eighteenth century periods. Several of the illustrations included in this series (Volume IX, Chapter 9) may be used to demonstrate the record in this particular. In every case, they exhibit an interest of texture that— secured by the use of irregular brick units, early bond variations, and varied joint treatments—

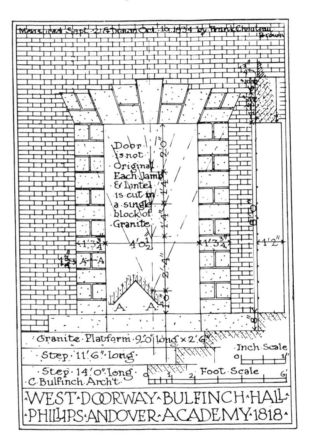

contains material for the study and consideration of architects appreciative of maintaining the variety and values of historic periods of craftsmanship in masonry, or to avail themselves of the inherited traditions of that trade, and apply them to modern problems of architectural design.

Structures dating from the earlier years of the nineteenth century, on the other hand, exhibit another aspect, also valuable and suggestive to the modern designer. A study of the several buildings by Charles Bulfinch, for instance—and perhaps most particularly the building at Phillips Andover called by his name—is illuminating from the severity and chastity of their design, as well as the extreme simplicity and reserve of their moulding treatment and ornamental embellishment.

Very probably this may have been the result of the requirement of economy imposed upon their designer by the conditions under which he was working at the time; of the need of these institutions to secure the utmost possible amount of building for the least possible amount of expenditure (a problem not very far removed from that confronting the profession during these very current years of the twentieth century!). But, whatever the cause, the results secured have great interest and value for architectural designers today. For interests of texture in the wall, other values have been substituted that may not be as widely interesting or appealing; for the romantic tendencies evident in the earlier designs, there are now to be seen the greater fineness and reserve of a Greek-derived delicacy and precision of outline and composition of area that almost approaches "bareness" in its result. The resulting simplicity certainly requires more understanding and a finer appreciation of the problem of architectural design upon the part of the public than might have been expected to exist at that time, even in New England. Or it may be that it was a direct out-growth of the very social conditions then animating this section of North America; the natural expression in architecture of the civilization then being derived from the early years of the Republic; of the conditions of life and living then surrounding the developing mentality of the region that was to flower a little later in the school of literature and thought that was to achieve its fullest culmination in New England in the philosophy of Alcott, Thoreau, and Emerson!

BULFINCH HALL — 1818 — PHILLIPS ANDOVER ACADEMY, ANDOVER, MASSACHUSETTS

Charles Bulfinch, Architect

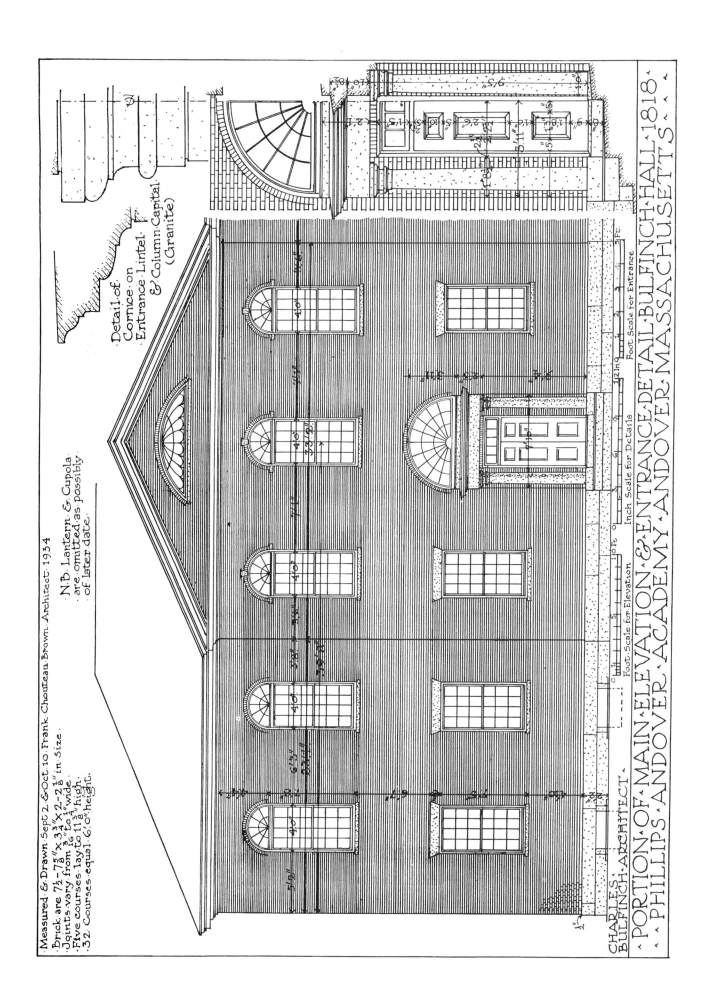

Measured & Drawn Sept 2 & Oct 10 Frank Choureau Brown Architect 1934

Brick are 7½–7⅞" × 3¾" × 2–2⅛" in Size.
Joints vary from 3⁄16" to 1" wide.
Five courses lay to 11⅜" high.
32 Courses equal 6'0" height.

N.B. Lantern & Cupola
are omitted as possibly
of later date.

Detail of
Cornice on
Entrance Lintel
& Column Capital.
(Granite)

CHARLES
BULFINCH ARCHITECT

PORTION OF MAIN ELEVATION & ENTRANCE DETAIL BULFINCH HALL 1818
PHILLIPS ANDOVER ACADEMY ANDOVER MASSACHUSETTS

PEARSON HALL—1817—PHILLIPS ANDOVER ACADEMY, ANDOVER, MASSACHUSETTS

UNIVERSITY HALL — 1815 — HARVARD UNIVERSITY, CAMBRIDGE, MASSACHUSETTS
Charles Bulfinch, Architect

HOLDEN CHAPEL—1744—HARVARD UNIVERSITY, CAMBRIDGE, MASSACHUSETTS

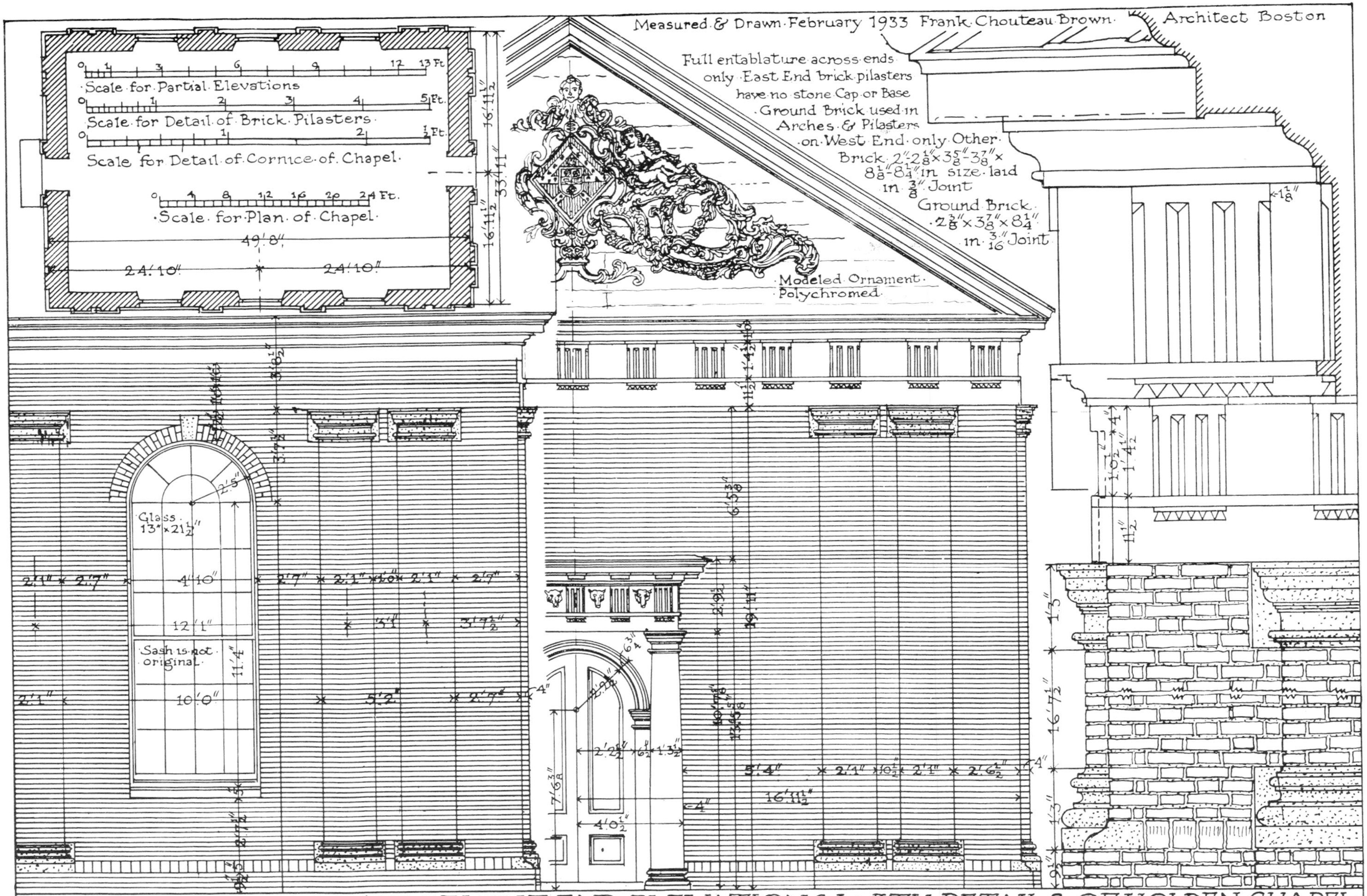

Measured & Drawn February 1933 Frank Chouteau Brown Architect Boston
Full entablature across ends only East End brick pilasters have no stone Cap or Base
Ground Brick used in Arches & Pilasters on West End only Other Brick 2"-2⅛" x 3⅝"-3⅞" x 8⅛"-8¼" in size laid in ⅜" Joint
Ground Brick 2⅜" x 3⅞" x 8¼" in 3/16" Joint
Modeled Ornament Polychromed
Scale for Partial Elevations
Scale for Detail of Brick Pilasters
Scale for Detail of Cornice of Chapel
Scale for Plan of Chapel
Glass 13" x 21½"
Sash is not original

PART NORTH SIDE & HALF OF WEST END ELEVATIONS WITH DETAILS OF HOLDEN CHAPEL BUILT IN 1744 IN HARVARD UNIVERSITY YARD AT CAMBRIDGE MASSACHUSETTS U S A

Group of Buildings

AMHERST COLLEGE, AMHERST, MASSACHUSETTS

GRIFFIN HALL, WILLIAMS COLLEGE, WILLIAMSTOWN, MASSACHUSETTS

UNIVERSITY HALL—1773—BROWN UNIVERSITY, PROVIDENCE, RHODE ISLAND

HOPE COLLEGE — 1825 — BROWN UNIVERSITY, PROVIDENCE, RHODE ISLAND

Colonial Public Buildings
in Salem, Massachusetts

Text by
M. S. Franklin
Photographs by
Arthur C. Haskell
Originally published in 1932 as White Pine Monograph
Volume XVIII, Number 3

CUSTOM HOUSE—1819—SALEM, MASSACHUSETTS
Measured drawings of porch, doorway, and Palladian window on pages 136–137.

PUBLIC BUILDINGS OF SALEM, MASSACHUSETTS

SALEM, the shire town of Essex County, Massachusetts, was first settled by a group under Roger Conant, who came on to Naumkeag (Salem) after a brief attempt to colonize upon the rocky shores of Cape Ann, under authority of the "Sheffield Patent" for settling the north shore of Massachusetts Bay. In September, 1628, another group of colonists, under Captain John Endecott, arrived bearing a new charter granted to the "Dorchester Company." And finally, Winthrop and his following, including Simon Bradstreet, arrived in June of 1630.

The first occupants of Salem became fishermen, while at Salem Village (now Danvers, the location of the "witchcraft delusion" of 1692) farming was also carried on. The outbreak of the Revolutionary War caused Salem, in 1776 a town of 5,337 inhabitants, to turn to privateering; and during the war the small community sent out a total of 158 vessels, manned by over 2000 men who brought back 445 prizes, more than half of those captured during the entire war! Thus was her maritime supremacy established, and the shipping was turned to commercial ventures at the end of the war, extending American commerce to new places and far distant seas; and bringing to the Salem of 1800 a population of 9,457 and the wealthiest merchant class of the New England coastal towns. After the embargo was placed upon American ports in 1808, our foreign commerce fell away, but in 1820 Salem had a population of 12,731; and it is within these years that the examples of architecture here selected for portrayal were all designed.

Derby Street, running along the margin of the Harbor, was in olden times the very center of the teeming maritime life of the community. Upon the one side were the old wharves, lined with shipping, extending out into the water; upon the other the houses, warehouses, and shops of the ship-owners. Nearby were the homes of their ship-captains and crews. Many a corner and wharfhead, too, had its tavern serving the grog and rum for which Salem was then almost as famous as Medford was later to become.

To get an idea of the wide variety of the cargoes brought from all over the world to the Salem of those days, one must now go to the crowded cases and walls of the Peabody Marine Museum on Essex Street, where many of these rare and colorful objects have been preserved along with models of the old ships, contemporary pictures of them and their exploits, and some of their old figureheads as well.

It is on Derby Street, opposite the head of Derby Wharf, that the Custom House, built in 1819, stands —though since 1913 the port has no longer its own collector. The building previously used for the purpose was burned in the great fire of October 6, 1774, along with many valuable records of the office. Joseph Hiller was the first collector under the Constitution, 1789–1801. Gen. James Miller, "the hero of Lundy's Lane," was collector from 1825 to 1849, and lived in the fine brick house adjoining at the left, built in 1811 by Benjamin Crowninshield, who was Secretary of the Navy under both Madison and Monroe. It was from 1846–1849 that Hawthorne came from the Old Manse at Concord to serve as "surveyor" at Salem. Another name, of interest this particular year, is William Fairfax, who came to Salem from Nassau as Royal Collector, but gave up the office to go to Virginia to act as manager of Lord Fairfax's vast estates, and live at Belvoir adjoining Mount Vernon; where his daughter married Lawrence Washington, and his son became the best friend of the young George Washington, accompanying him on his surveying expedition into the Ohio valley.

Although of too late a date to have been the work of Samuel McIntire, who died in 1811, the finely moulded ornament, the spirited capitals of the porch columns, and especially the lifelike carving of the eagle adorning the roof balustrade of the Custom House show the influence of that master carver upon the school succeeding him in his home locality. Despite the late date, the richness of handling of the more architectural portions of the structure are still notable examples of the fine feeling for beauty and richness, combined with restraint and simplicity, that is illustrated by the best New England architecture of this period. Compare the essential simplicity of the interior treatment of the entrance doorway and its spacious side and fanlights, with the more florid detail of its exterior face, and one can realize the fine straight-thinking craftsmanship that combined so successfully the two designs. The bricks are a rather full height, laid in a narrow joint averaging an eighth inch in thickness, in Flemish bond; with refined wooden mouldings, some of which show the flattened Greek tendency in their outline. The sidelights of both Palladian window and door originally had patterns marked in thin eight-inch wood strips between the heavier muntins.

Within the hallway, the simple staircase rises to second floor and roof cupola—where the outlook always kept watch over the harbor entrance—and a tall archway leads to the stores in the rear, while the five doorways on the main floor are handled with the simplest of characteristic finish and entablature. The naïve manner in which the doorhead under the curving stairway has been truncated so as not to interfere with the detail of the stair ends, while still conforming so far as may be with the neighboring doorhead, is also worthy of attention.

While many visit the Custom House because of the few years that it was housing the famous author, Hawthorne, yet it has probably but seldom received the attention today that its architectural features merit; even though its location is but a short half-mile from the center of the city.

Recalling the many controversies waged over the locations and sizes of early theatre buildings in the United States, it is odd that it is in Puritan New England that we find still extant an edifice of sixty by ninety feet, built in 1828 as Salem's first theatre—though it was in actual use for only four years. By that time the curse invoked by certain pious inhabitants who, according to tradition, knelt one night upon the piles of lumber and bricks going into the new structure to pray that God would soon bring to ruin this "diabolical venture," had its effect. Despite the acting of Junius Booth and Edwin Forrest, business did not prosper and the building became "dark." So, in 1832, when Rufus Choate and some others from the Howard Street, or Branch Church, wanted to set up a new Congregational Society, this building was secured, the stage torn out, a pulpit installed in its place, and it was dedicated on November 22, 1832 to its new uses. The hundredth anniversary is being celebrated this year.

With the exception of the upper portion of the gable, including the tablet bearing the later date, the façade seems to have been very little changed. Designed in two planes of brick surfaces, one set four inches back of the other, the building still remains a direct and convincingly simple expression of the architectural methods of the time.

But the theatre was not the only indication of a certain carnal-mindedness upon the part of the old Salemites; for if architecture is a true expression of the life of a people, a study of the architectural remains still found in the town would seem to proclaim unusual fondness for another means of self expression usually supposed to have been frowned upon by the Puritan—dancing! And incidentally, it would also seem to have been rampant among the same group who were even then upholding, with others of aristocratic background, the tenets of Federalism.

How otherwise may one explain what is now called the Assembly House, which was built in 1782 as a Federalist Clubhouse, with a hall used for concerts, balls, plays, dances, and oratorios from then until 1795. Lafayette was entertained here on October 29, 1784, and Washington October 29, 1789. Shortly after that date it was altered into a dwelling. The porch was added—the graceful vine scrolled along the architrave is among the many details attributed to Samuel McIntire (1757–1811)—and the interior so changed that it is difficult now to establish the original arrangement. The Federal Club building, with its grouped pilasters somewhat suggesting its more imposing public character, remains upon its exterior, at least, a pleasing example of early New England formal architecture.

Hamilton Hall was built in 1805 from plans by Samuel McIntire and presents its more imposing side elevation to Chestnut Street. The front, with a spreading pediment, is very severe, hardly suggesting its festal character; which is expressed, however, along the side, with its five groups of Palladian windows, and the panels above, with the characteristic eagle adorning the central location. Inside, the hall itself is upon the second floor, and is square in plan, with a curved or arched plaster ceiling. The detail is again very simply carried out; with pilasters, without entasis, upon the walls. The sparsely narrowed window groups, of refined yet restricted detail, are related to the wall seating in a most engaging yet architectural manner; and, finally, the overhanging music balcony, with its gracefully curved line, and simple balustrade, even omits the usual strengthening buttress at the external angles. The interior is so restrained, almost bare, that the old gilt mirrors and handsome chandelier and wall brackets appear quite florid by contrast. Again its naming after Alexander Hamilton, the leader

CUSTOM HOUSE — 1819 — SALEM, MASSACHUSETTS

A — A

B — B   C — C   FOR DETAILS   E — E

D — D

0   1   2   3   4   5 INS

0   1   2   3 FEET

ONE·HALF·EXTERIOR·&·ONE·HALF·INTERIOR·ELEVATION·
MEASURED·&·DRAWN·BY· FRANK·CHOUTEAU·BROWN·

MAY·1932

·ENTRANCE·DOOR·AND·ARCHWAY·
·CUSTOM·HOUSE·1819·SALEM·MASSACHUSETTS·

Doors Modern

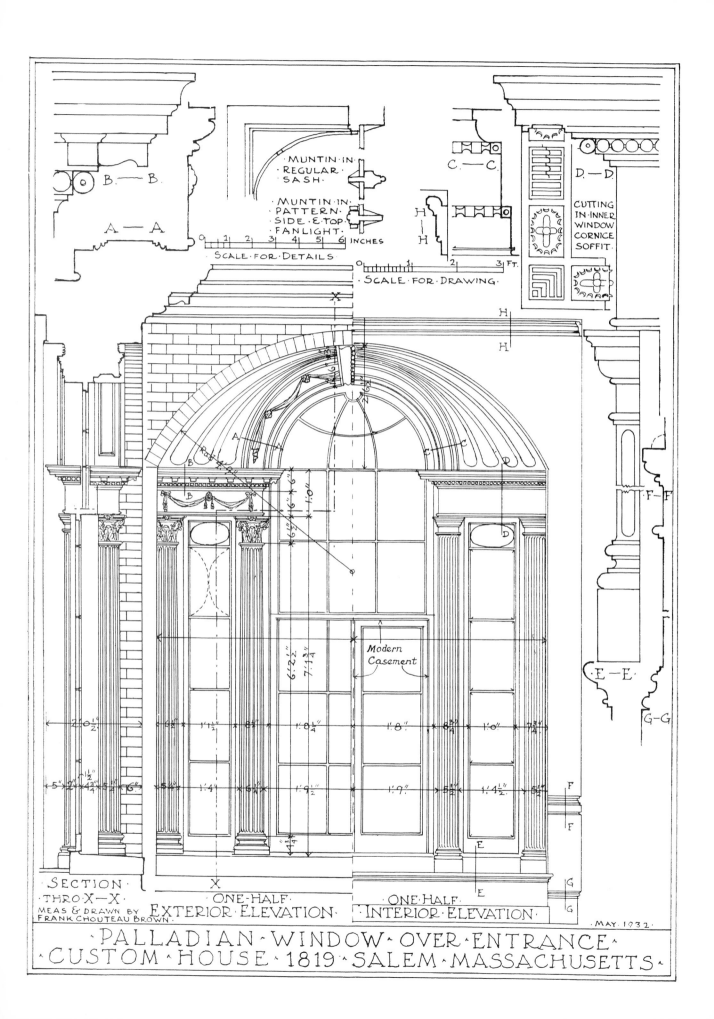

B — B.

A — A.

MUNTIN·IN·
REGULAR·
SASH.

MUNTIN·IN·
PATTERN·
SIDE·&·TOP·
FANLIGHT.

0 1 2 3 4 5 6 INCHES
·SCALE·FOR·DETAILS·

0 1 2 3½ FT.
·SCALE·FOR·DRAWING·

C. — C.

H — H

D. — D.

CUTTING·
IN·INNER·
WINDOW·
CORNICE·
SOFFIT.

F — F

E — E.

G — G

Modern
Casement

SECTION·
THRO·X—X·
MEAS·&·DRAWN·BY
FRANK·CHOUTEAU·BROWN·

·ONE·HALF·
EXTERIOR·ELEVATION·

·ONE·HALF·
INTERIOR·ELEVATION·

MAY·1932·

·PALLADIAN·WINDOW·OVER·ENTRANCE·
·CUSTOM·HOUSE·1819·SALEM·MASSACHUSETTS·

Window Detail
CUSTOM HOUSE—1819—SALEM, MASSACHUSETTS

Hallway
CUSTOM HOUSE — 1819 — SALEM, MASSACHUSETTS
The necessarily truncated doorhead conforms otherwise with its neighbor.

ASSEMBLY HOUSE — 1782 — SALEM, MASSACHUSETTS

HAMILTON HALL—1805—CHESTNUT STREET, SALEM, MASSACHUSETTS
Samuel McIntire, Architect

Hall

HAMILTON HALL—1805—SALEM, MASSACHUSETTS

Side Elevation
HAMILTON HALL—1805—SALEM, MASSACHUSETTS
Detail of Chestnut Street façade. The hall on second floor expressed by groups of Palladian windows.

of the Federalist party, which was so strong between 1793 and 1820, indicates the proclivities of the better Salem families of that time.

It remains to record a third "Hall," important in old Salem records. It was known as Washington Hall, and was dedicated February 22, 1793—the birthday of Washington that marked his second assumption of the presidency—with a dinner and speeches including much gratification at the recently received news of the French Revolution. Its main characteristics are shown in the single old photograph reproduced from the records of the Essex Institute.

inal appearance of another example of Bulfinch's work may still be obtained from a visit to the city almshouse, out upon the Neck, built in 1816.

All these later buildings express, with others of their time, an innate restraint, not almost to say meagreness and thinness of detail, accompanied by great delicacy of moulding outline, and a tendency that may be noted in several of these examples to substitute reeding for fluting or paneling in the pilaster faces. The Almshouse was probably also a problem in economics, as the great number of shiftless seafaring men then making Salem their homeport, necessitated

Photograph by Courtesy of Essex Institute, Salem, Mass.

WASHINGTON HALL—1793—SALEM, MASSACHUSETTS
Formerly located in the third story of building at 101 Washington Street.

The building itself has disappeared. It was used for all sorts of social gatherings, as were the other halls illustrated—and in later years came into use as a theatre as well.

The name of Charles Bulfinch comes into the architectural records of Salem upon several occasions. He was among those who made sketches for the famous town house of Elias Hasket Derby, built upon the site of the present market hall, in 1799, by Samuel McIntire. In 1811, Bulfinch designed the building on Central Street for the Essex Bank, still standing, though in a much altered state. An idea of the orig-

that a structure of considerable size be planned. This five-storied structure was the result, and it was considered so successful that it was visited by President Monroe when he came to Salem in 1817. It lacks entirely any central feature, which the designer tried to supply by advancing the central part of the structure *en échelon*, with a doorway upon the main floor at each side. The result is an ingenious yet very simple design, but little known. It is finely situated, overlooking a stretch of open water fronting toward Beverly Harbor and the Northern Shore of Massachusetts Bay.

FIRST THEATRE — 1828 — SALEM, MASSACHUSETTS
Dedicated as a church in 1832, since which the façade has been little changed.

ALMSHOUSE — 1816 — SALEM NECK, MASSACHUSETTS
Charles Bulfinch, Architect

Interior Treatment of
Period Windows

Text by
Frank Chouteau Brown
Photographs by
Arthur C. Haskell
Originally published in 1932 as White Pine Monograph
Volume XVIII, Number 5

Circular Topped Window on Staircase Landing
"THE LINDENS"—1754—FORMERLY AT DANVERS, MASSACHUSETTS

SOME EXAMPLES OF PERIOD WINDOWS
WITH DETAILS OF THEIR INTERIOR TREATMENT

IN the North American colonies, the double-hung type of window came into use gradually from shortly after the beginning of the eighteenth century. We have knowledge of structures, built in the first years after 1700, with the casement framed sash (Volume IX, Chapter 13) then still in use, but probably by about 1720 to 1735 the newer double-hung sash style had been generally accepted, and the older buildings were being gradually changed over to agree with the new English fashion.

By then, too, many of the glassworks on the new continent were becoming proficient enough to manufacture window glass that, while it still contained many imperfections in thickness and surface, was yet becoming commercially available in sizes that were growing gradually larger and clearer during the balance of that century until—by the early years of the nineteenth—glass areas as large as 12 x 15 to 12 x 18 inches were in common use. By that time, too, the usually proportioned window openings were customarily being fitted with two sash, each probably having six lights, thus filling the entire opening with twelve lights of glass, three wide and four high. This arrangement and proportion continued to be employed until well into the latter half of that century, when windows having only four—or even, finally, but two—glazed areas, came into the market.

But with the period with which we are now concerned—the hundred years extending from about 1720 to 1820—the double-hung sash window was gradually increasing in its dimensions, along with the gradually enlarging rooms of the Georgian house, and the considerably higher ceilings that were then coming into vogue. In many cases the older dwellings, into which these new window frames were being built, had not previously been finished inside other than by walls faced with featheredged boards, even if they had not even been left without any inside surface finish whatever, as had often been the case with the first built structures. It was, therefore, comparatively easy to insert the new window frames, with

their two sliding sash, and then—or a little later—refinish the entire interior with the different styles of paneled walls and dadoes; or the plaster walls and ceilings that were then beginning to be copied from the more imposing mansions of Georgian England. And this inner plaster facing, when it was added, could as easily be furred in some eight or ten more inches, thus completely concealing the heavy upright corner posts still found in the house framing and at the same time setting the window within a recess, the sloping and paneled reveals of which were in many cases the very shutters closing over the opening, now arranged to fold back upon either side when not in use. These shutters took the place of those that had previously hung exposed, as in the Short House (page 151), or slid back into the space at one or both sides of the window opening, as in the Wentworth House (page 159).

The very earliest and simplest type of double-hung window is, perhaps, only represented by the single example of the dormer treatment shown upon the next page. In the small early cottage, the nicest possible adjustment of harmony in scale and composition is essential for their successful employment, both within and without the building. No attempt has been made, in this chapter, to cover other than the usual window usage, save in a couple of examples of stairway landing windows, both employing an arched, or semicircular, top. One is from the Sarah Orne Jewett House, pages 153 and 154; and the other, from the somewhat more pretentious "Lindens," formerly at Danvers, Massachusetts, is shown on pages 148 and 152.

In other cases, this central second hall window is only marked by being somewhat shorter or longer than others with which it lines upon the house exterior, except in those cases where it provides an outlet, perhaps, upon a porch roof or balcony, as happens with the example from the Woodbridge-Short House, at Salem (pages 157 and 158), where the third sash was introduced to obtain the length necessary for that purpose.

A considerable part of the interior effectiveness of these windows depended upon the importance of their moulded or recessed framing. In earlier and simpler examples this was often very slight—sometimes the wooden reveal of the opening ended only with a beaded edge, left projecting slightly beyond the plaster wall face. Often the facing was widened by another strip of moulded finish. Sometimes this framing of the window opening was extended down to the floor below or connected with the cornice above. In the first case, a different panel of woodwork, or perhaps a seat fitted into the recess, might fill the space beneath the window. Or the bottom of the window might line with the top of a plain wooden dado carried about the room (pages 155, 158 or 161); or even break down into a higher dado, to fit into its paneled arrangement (page 154). Where the window trim did not merely cope into the cornice above; where it was mitred across over the top of the opening, or brought up against the under side of the cornice with an intermediate frieze; the cornice might be broken out to mark more distinctly the window location. It was then often broken out in a similar manner over a door, or mantel, upon another side of the room, even when it had no actual physical connection with either one.

All this emphasis of the interior architectural framing of the window opening was a gradual development that accompanied the greater wealth of the new builders and owners of homes in the principal coastal cities of the colonies, but still did not much affect the continuing use of the simpler, earlier forms of double-hung windows in the smaller villages, cottages, and farmhouses of the countryside. There the older low ceilings continued in use, and the smaller scaled glass areas that were relative to their more modest dimensions continued to be employed; and so the smaller glass sizes were carried along in use up to a comparatively late time, just as they were, during the same period, gradually increasing in size and diminishing

Interior of Recessed Dormer Window
HOUSE AT HEAD OF THE COVE—BEFORE 1750—
ANNISQUAM, MASSACHUSETTS

in number, in the larger and more pretentious dwellings of pre-Revolutionary and Revolutionary times.

In the illustration on page 161, showing the window and curtaining from a chamber in the Concord Antiquarian House, the window, which is glazed with twenty-four small lights, does not extend to touch the McIntire type cornice at the top of the wall, although it is treated in the manner characteristic of his work of about 1810–1811 in Salem—even though there usually employed in rooms of more ample height. The recess and the side architraves framing the opening are carried down to the floor below. The bottom of the window still lines with the top of the plain dado design, but the space above the window panel under the opening (which also lines in height with the cap of the dado) is enriched with a jig-sawn pattern applied upon the wood back—as was so often

Twenty-Four-Light Window in First Story Room
SHORT HOUSE — c1732 — OLD NEWBURY, MASSACHUSETTS

woven fabric that was known as India muslin in the time of Sheraton, from whom this treatment has been adapted.

In addition to providing examples of their architectural treatment, and showing the window opening in relation to its surrounding wall areas, as the illustrations have been selected to do, a certain number also indicate some of the several methods and styles of curtaining that are appropriate to the different periods of their design. As a general rule, it might be stated that in a house of any authentic Colonial period, the simpler the decorative treatment the more successful and satisfying is generally the result. This applies especially to the selection and arrangement of the drapery in or about the window openings.

If too heavy, it destroys the proportion and structural framing of the opening, as well as obscures the light. If too light, it may appear skimpy or meagre; although under rather than over-elaboration is always to be preferred! Some windows, especially of the earlier periods, are the better for the omission of colored curtaining altogether. And, above all, nothing so quickly and entirely destroys the directness

McIntire's custom with his decoration, whether sawn or carved — as it may be seen in the Woodbridge-Short and Pingree, or other of the houses in Salem of his later design.

The curtaining of this window, while it entirely hides all the enframing wooden trim about the recessed opening (rather a pity, when well conceived and proportioned!) is yet nevertheless to be approved for its restraint in pattern and arrangement. As shown here it is made of a plain dusty blue stuff, velvet-like in quality, and sufficiently thin to take pleasant folds where back-tied with strips of the same velvet. It hangs from behind a formal boxed heading of the material, emphasized by a braided outline, while it is set off by an equally simple pair of muslin sash curtains (often advisedly omitted in formal Georgian rooms of heavier design), suggesting the sheer

and dignity of formal early American interiors, as an over-draped and eccentric arrangement of the material — except perhaps the use of over-emphasized and incongruous brocaded patterns, or an over brilliant and glaring color contrast, either in the material or with the walls and color scheme otherwise dominating the room. Even the most elaborately detailed authentic Georgian interiors of pre-Revolutionary date are usually much bettered by the simplest of window curtaining, or equally injured by the addition of unnecessary fripperies. Particularly in these days, when careful analysis and research are disclosing that white was neither invariably the original paint color applied over the interior trim, nor paper even the usual original treatment of the walls! We now know that later fashions have covered a mass of early coloring on walls and woodwork.

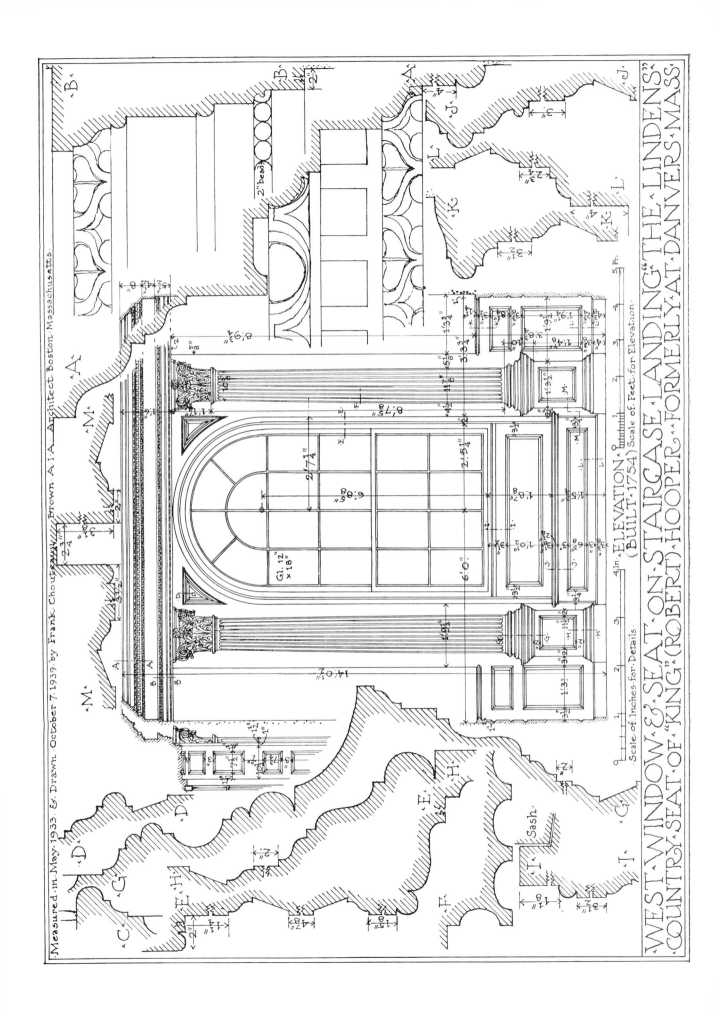

WEST·WINDOW·&·SEAT·ON·STAIRCASE·LANDING·"THE·LINDENS"
COUNTRY·SEAT·OF·"KING"·(ROBERT)·HOOPER··FORMERLY·AT·DANVERS·MASS·

·ELEVATION·   (BUILT·1754)·Scale·of·Feet·for·Elevation·

·Measured·in·May·1933·&·Drawn·October·7·1939·by·Frank·Chouteau·Brown·A.I.A.·Architect·Boston·Massachusetts·

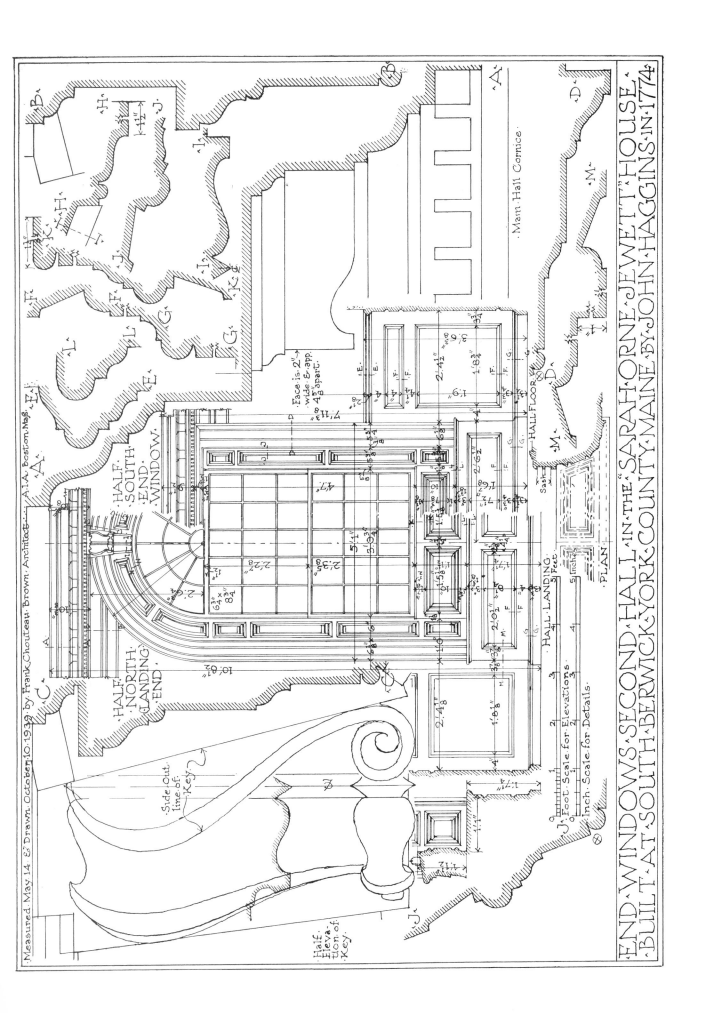

Measured. May. 14 . & Drawn. October. 10. 1939. by. Frank. Chouteau. Brown. Architect . . A.I.A. Boston. Mass.

Half. South. End. Window.

Half. North. Landing. End.

Side. Out . line. of . Key.

Half. Elevation. of . Key.

Mam. Hall Cornice.

Hall Floor.

Sash.

Hall. Landing.

PLAN.

Face is. 2″ wide & app. 4⅝″ apart.

J. Foot. Scale for. Elevations.
5 Feet

Inch. Scale for. Details.
5 inches

END. WINDOWS. SECOND. HALL. IN. THE. "SARA. HORNE. JEWETT" HOUSE.
BUILT. AT. SOUTH. BERWICK. YORK. COUNTY. MAINE. BY. JOHN. HAGGINS. IN. 1774.

Front Window, Second Hall
SARAH ORNE JEWETT HOUSE—1774—SO. BERWICK, MAINE

Window on Staircase Landing
SARAH ORNE JEWETT HOUSE—1774—SO. BERWICK, MAINE

Window in South Parlor

GEN. SALEM TOWNE HOUSE—1796—CHARLTON,
MASSACHUSETTS

Window in Living Room

BEZALEEL MANN HOUSE—1790—NORTH ATTLEBOROUGH,
MASSACHUSETTS

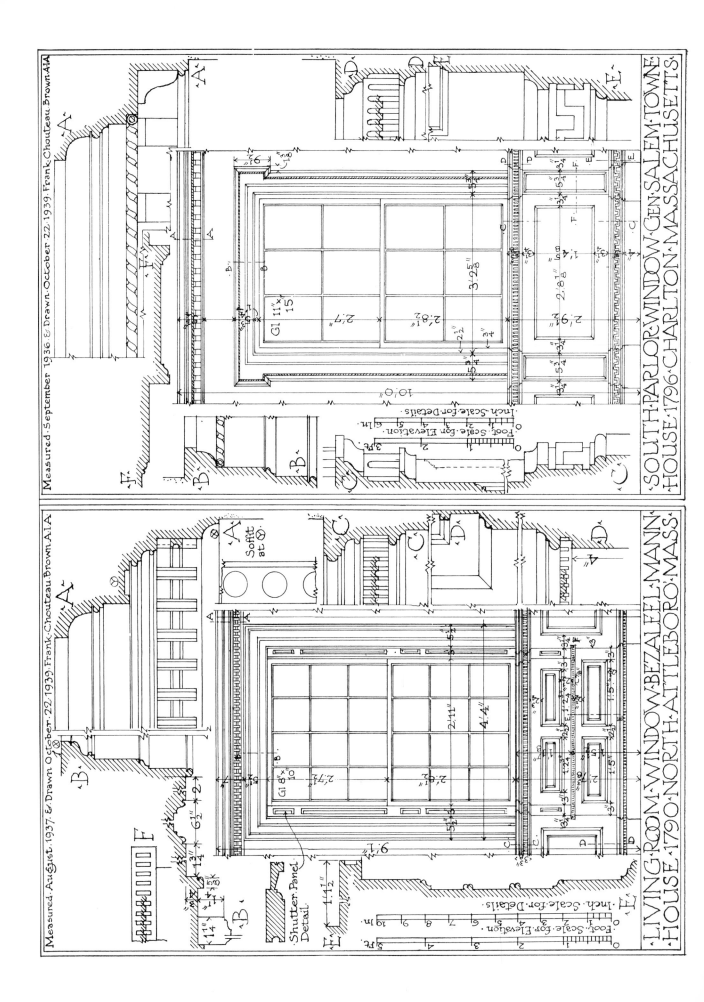

·SOUTH·PARLOR·WINDOW·GEN·SALEM·TOWNE·
·HOUSE·1796·CHARLTON·MASSACHUSETTS·

·LIVING·ROOM·WINDOW·BEZALEEL·MANN·
·HOUSE·1790·NORTH·ATTLEBORO·MASS·

Measured·September·1936·&·Drawn·October·22·1939·Frank·Chouteau·Brown·AIA·

Measured·August·1937·&·Drawn·October·22·1939·Frank·Chouteau·Brown·AIA·

Inch·Scale·For·Details·

Foot·Scale·for·Elevation·

Shutter·Panel·
Detail·

Soffit
at ⊗

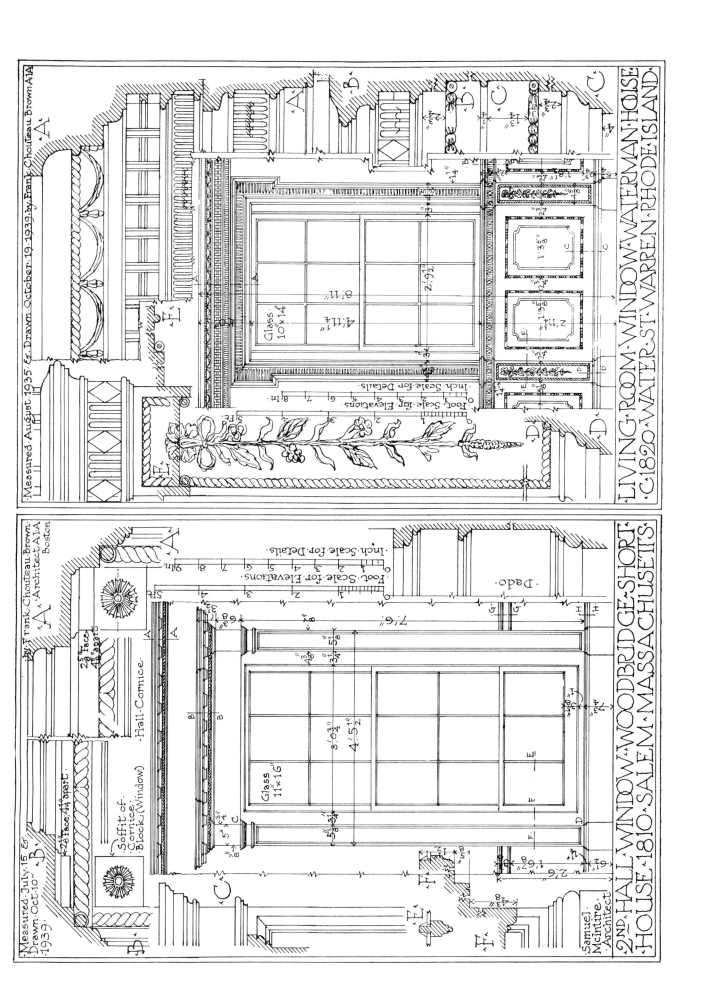

Measured August 1935 & Drawn October 19 1939 by Frank Chouteau Brown AIA

Glass 10"×14"

4'11¼"

8'11"

2'·9½"

Inch·Scale·for·Details
Foot·Scale·for·Elevations

1'·3⅝"

2'·1¼"

LIVING·ROOM·WINDOW·WATERMAN·HOUSE·
·C1820·WATER·ST·WARREN·RHODE·ISLAND·

·by·Frank·Chouteau·Brown·
·A·Architect·AIA·
·Boston·

2⅝"·face·4½"·apart

2⅜"·face·4½"·apart

·Soffit·of·
·Cornice·
·Block·(Window)

·Hall·Cornice·

Inch·Scale·for·Details
Foot·Scale·for·Elevations

·Dado·

Glass 11"×16"

8'·0¾"

4'·5½"

7'·6"

Measured·July·15·&·
Drawn·Oct·10·
1939·

·Samuel·
·McIntire·
·Architect·

2ND·HALL·WINDOW·WOODBRIDGE·SHORT·
·HOUSE·1810·SALEM·MASSACHUSETTS·

Window in Living Room
WATERMAN HOUSE—c1820—WARREN,
RHODE ISLAND

Front Window in Second Hall
WOODBRIDGE-SHORT HOUSE—1810—SALEM,
MASSACHUSETTS

Window in Pine Parlor

COL. PAUL WENTWORTH MANSION—1701—SALMON FALLS,
NEW HAMPSHIRE

Corner of Front Parlor

RICHARD DERBY HOUSE—1761—DERBY STREET, SALEM,
MASSACHUSETTS

Fifteen-Light Windows in Parlor End, Later Portion
ELIAS ENDICOTT PORTER FARMHOUSE—c1815—DANVERS, MASSACHUSETTS

Windows in South Chamber
JOHN TURNER HOUSE (SEVEN GABLES)—1668—SALEM, MASSACHUSETTS

Twenty-Four-Light Window and Draperies of Early Nineteenth Century
ANTIQUARIAN HOUSE, CONCORD, MASSACHUSETTS

Window in Living Room

DR. PETER OLIVER HOUSE—1762—MIDDLEBOROUGH, MASSACHUSETTS

Window in Living Room

DURANT-KENRICK HOUSE—1732—NEWTON, MASSACHUSETTS

Early Interior Doorways
in New England

Text by
Arthur C. Haskell
Photographs by
The Author
Originally published in 1939 as White Pine Monograph
Volume XVIII, Number 5

Batten Doors to Kitchen Closet and Entry
HASKELL HOUSE — 1652 — WEST GLOUCESTER, MASSACHUSETTS

EARLY INTERIOR DOORWAYS IN NEW ENGLAND

THE simplest form of early door was made of one or two wide wooden boards, fastened to cross battens or ledger boards placed across the back, usually six or seven inches down from the top and about eight to ten inches up from the bottom of the door, and generally nailed with old hand-forged iron nails, which were driven through from the face and clinched by having the pointed end hammered over upon the back of the batten. As the earliest houses were enclosed by nailing or pinning upright boards against the frame outside from sill to plate, it was natural at first to build interior partitions in the same way; cutting doors through wherever they were wanted and making the door from the pieces cut out of the upright boarding, by fitting them against battens placed across the back, usually coming on either the closet, kitchen or hall side of the opening. This sort of a door was strengthened by the use of long flat wrought iron hinges, known as "strap" hinges, often extending almost entirely across the door, and always for about two-thirds of its width. These were usually nailed with hand-made nails clinched on the back, and placed over the batten, so that the boards were held firmly between the wooden batten on the back and the flat iron strap upon the face; and every board carried two or more of the nails to help brace and stiffen the door's construction. Sometimes the battens were moulded along the edge, with a quarter round or mould like the one shown in the drawing; sometimes the crosspieces were connected by upright members along each edge, making almost a frame or panel upon the back; sometimes they were braced by a diagonal brace or strut starting on the hinged side at the top of the bottom crosspiece, to correct or prevent any tendency to sag along the outer edge of the door.

From these back-framed doors it was an easy step to the paneled door, with two or more panels, usually moulded upon only one face, with the moulding always worked along the inner edge of the stile; and therefore a part of it—in all old work. Two paneled doors were among the earlier framed types, but doors with a middle upright stile were evidently soon added; and from then on the arrangement and variety of the panels, and their varied proportions and shapes, become a fascinating study for those interested or concerned with the art of building.

There are many six paneled doors, with small cross panels placed either just below the middle of the door's height, or across the top. Sometimes one cross panel runs entirely across the door, although there may be two panels in its width elsewhere. Some early doors have the lower panel cross-braced, making four triangular panels. Sometimes both the upper and lower part of the door is framed in this way. Occasionally the lower part of the top cross stile has a circular segment taken out of it, giving the effect of an arch or curve to the outline of the upper panel; and this treatment is sometimes taken across an entire paneled end of a room—or again it is merely confined to the doors, or perhaps to a set of panels arranged across the space over the fireplace.

An eight paneled door, like that from the old Dillaway House, is rather a favorite in nicely built dwellings, and the panels are sometimes raised upon both faces, and the stiles also moulded, so that there is really no "back" to the door, but both sides are "faces." There are also ten paneled doors, with a small panel top and bottom, and one in the middle of its height—while still another entirely new grouping of panels becomes available when the door is given three panels in width, making a six, nine, or twelve paneled door—as in the case of the entrance to the old Governor Hancock House—depending upon the number of panels into which its height was divided.

In this section, dealing with early doors and their enframement, only the more usual types have been selected from these early examples. Once we turn into the eighteenth century, a few of the best houses provide us with instances of the fine craftsmanship and beautiful finish that the skill and pains taken by the workmen of that time together made possible. They present models that the most costly houses of today can hardly undertake to better, although examples of this kind increase in number and beauty of treatment as the century nears its end and turns the corner into the first twenty-five years of the nineteenth century.

The gradual progress in the methods and means by which doors were hung and fitted with hardware is almost as interesting as the gradual changes made in their design and construction. The earliest swinging valves were probably roughly fitted, and hung by

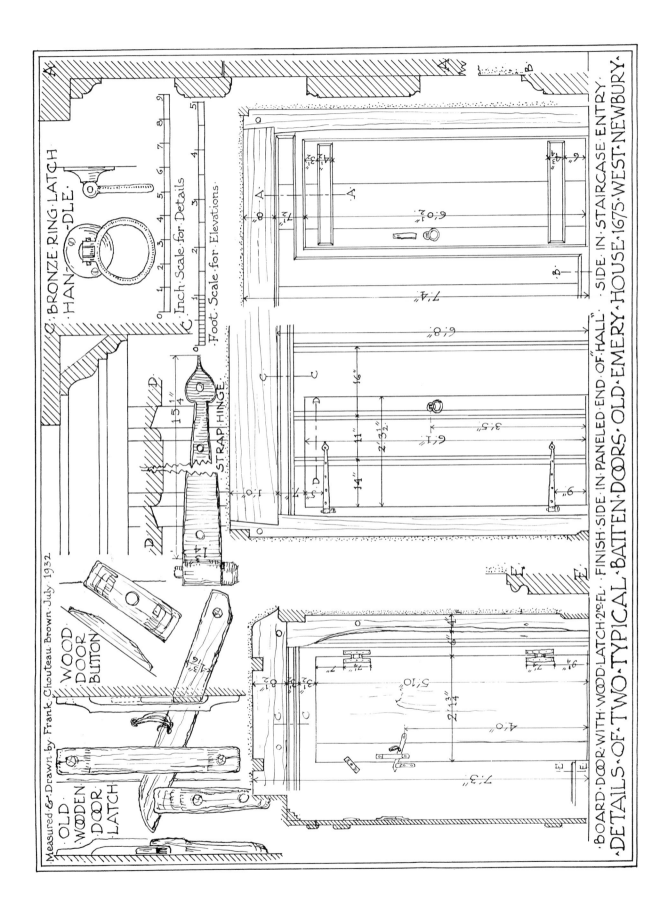

·C· BRONZE· RING· LATCH·
HAN— —DLE·

·Inch· Scale· for· Details·

·Foot· Scale· for· Elevations·

STRAP· HINGE·

WOOD
DOOR
BUTTON·

Measured· &· Drawn· by· Frank· Chouteau· Brown· July· 1932·

·OLD·
WOODEN·
DOOR·
LATCH·

·BOARD· DOOR· WITH· WOOD· LATCH· 2ᴺᴰ· FL· · FINISH· SIDE· IN· PANELED· END· OF· HALL· · SIDE· IN· STAIRCASE· ENTRY·

·DETAILS· OF· TWO· TYPICAL· BATTEN· DOORS· OLD· EMERY· HOUSE· 1675· WEST· NEWBURY·

Back of Batten (Staircase Entry Side) Door to Hall

Board Door with Wooden Latch, Second Floor

TYPICAL BATTEN DOORS FROM OLD EMERY HOUSE—1675—WEST NEWBURY, MASSACHUSETTS

Door in Second Hall
WAYSIDE INN — 1686 — SUDBURY, MASSACHUSETTS

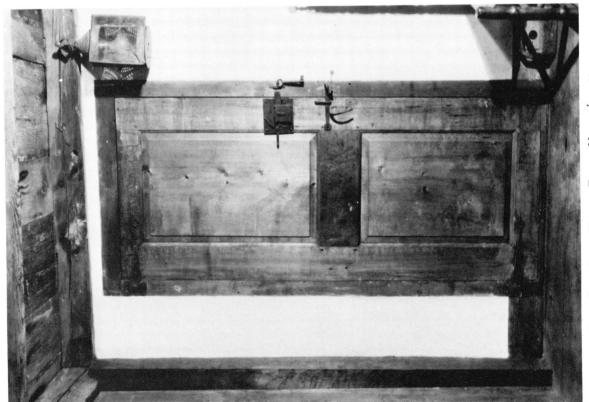

Door from Lane House, Essex, Massachusetts
HASKELL HOUSE — 1700 — WEST GLOUCESTER, MASSACHUSETTS

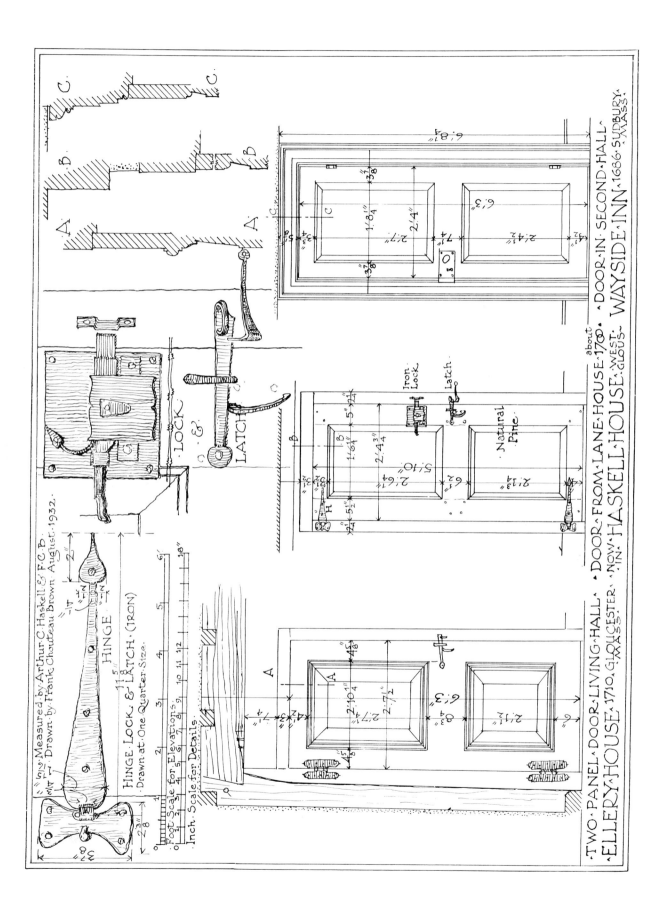

·LOCK·&·

·LATCH·

·HINGE·

·HINGE·LOCK·&·LATCH·(IRON)·
·Drawn·at·One·Quarter·Size·

·Foot·Scale·for·Elevations·

·Inch·Scale·for·Details·

·Measured·by·Arthur·C·Haskell·&·F.C.B·
·Drawn·by·Frank·Chouteau·Brown·August·1932·

·Natural·Pine·

·Iron·Lock·

·Latch·

·TWO·PANEL·DOOR·LIVING·HALL· ·DOOR·FROM·LANE·HOUSE·1700· ·DOOR·IN·SECOND·HALL·
·ELLERY·HOUSE·1710·GLOUCESTER·MASS· about ·HASKELL·HOUSE·WEST· ·WAYSIDE·INN·1686·SUDBURY·
·NOW·IN· ·GLOUS· ·MASS·

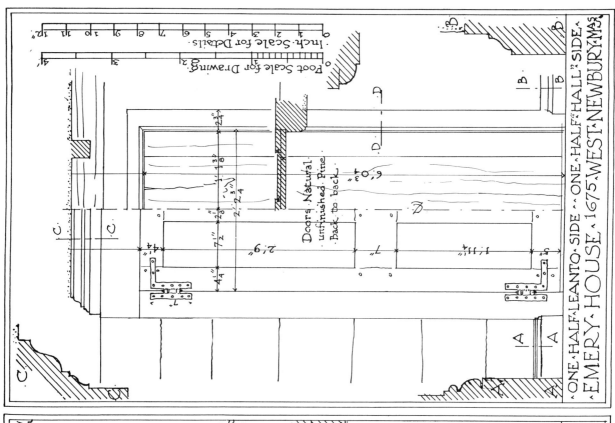

ONE·HALF·LEAN·TO·SIDE·· ONE·HALF·"HALL"SIDE· EMERY·HOUSE·1675·WEST·NEWBURY·MASS·

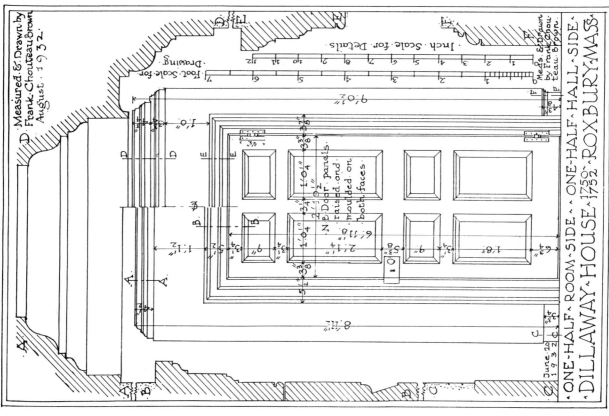

·ONE·HALF·ROOM·SIDE·· ONE·HALF·HALL·SIDE· DILLAWAY·HOUSE·1750·1752·ROXBURY·MASS·

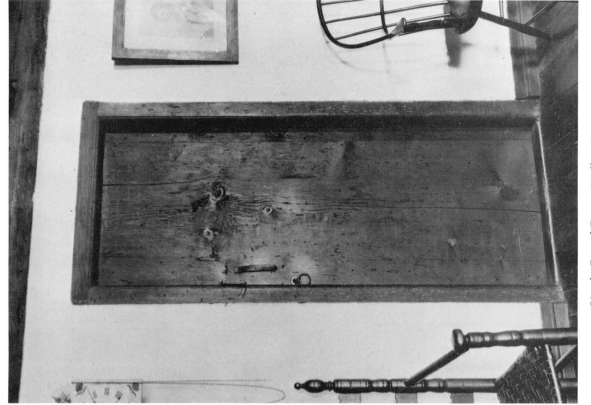

Single Board Door, Hall to Lean-to
EMERY HOUSE —1675— WEST NEWBURY, MASSACHUSETTS

Eight Paneled Door, Second Floor
DILLAWAY HOUSE —1750— ROXBURY, MASSACHUSETTS

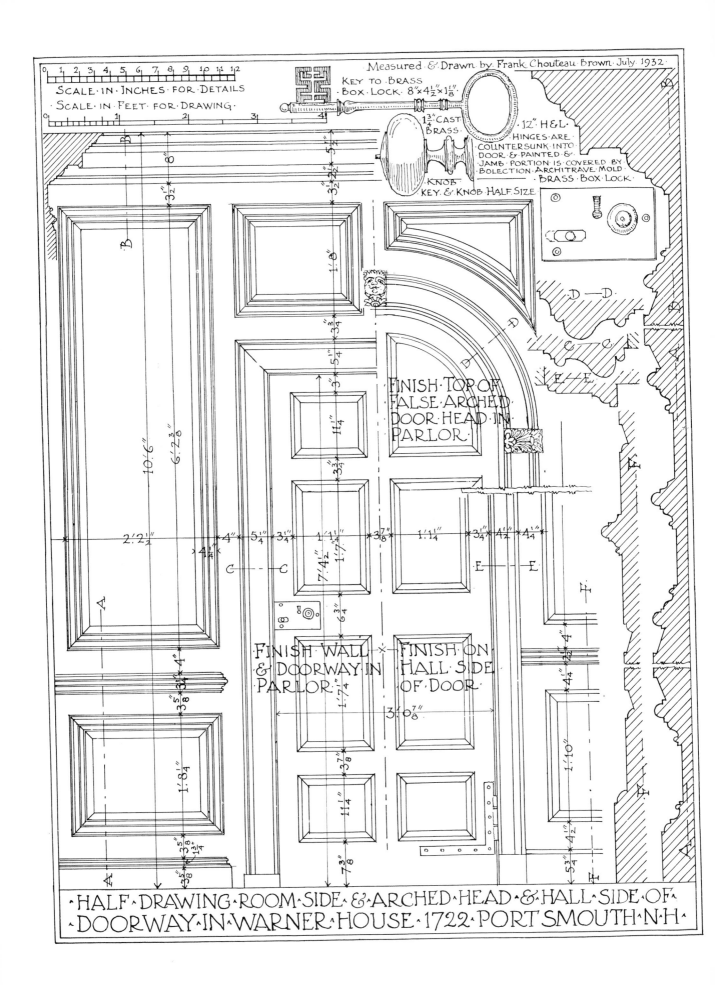

Measured & Drawn by Frank Chouteau Brown · July 1932

SCALE·IN·INCHES·FOR·DETAILS
·SCALE·IN·FEET·FOR·DRAWING·

KEY·TO·BRASS
BOX·LOCK· 8"×4½"×1⅛"

1¾"·CAST
BRASS·

12"·H&L·
HINGES·ARE·
COUNTERSUNK·INTO
DOOR·&·PAINTED·&·
JAMB·PORTION·IS·COVERED·BY
BOLECTION·ARCHITRAVE·MOLD
·BRASS·BOX·LOCK·

·KNOB·
·KEY·&·KNOB·HALF·SIZE·

·FINISH·TOP·OF·
·FALSE·ARCHED·
·DOOR·HEAD·IN·
·PARLOR·

·FINISH·WALL·
·&·DOORWAY·IN·
·PARLOR·

·FINISH·ON·
·HALL·SIDE·
·OF·DOOR·

·HALF·DRAWING·ROOM·SIDE·&·ARCHED·HEAD·&·HALL·SIDE·OF·
·DOORWAY·IN·WARNER·HOUSE·1722·PORTSMOUTH·N·H·

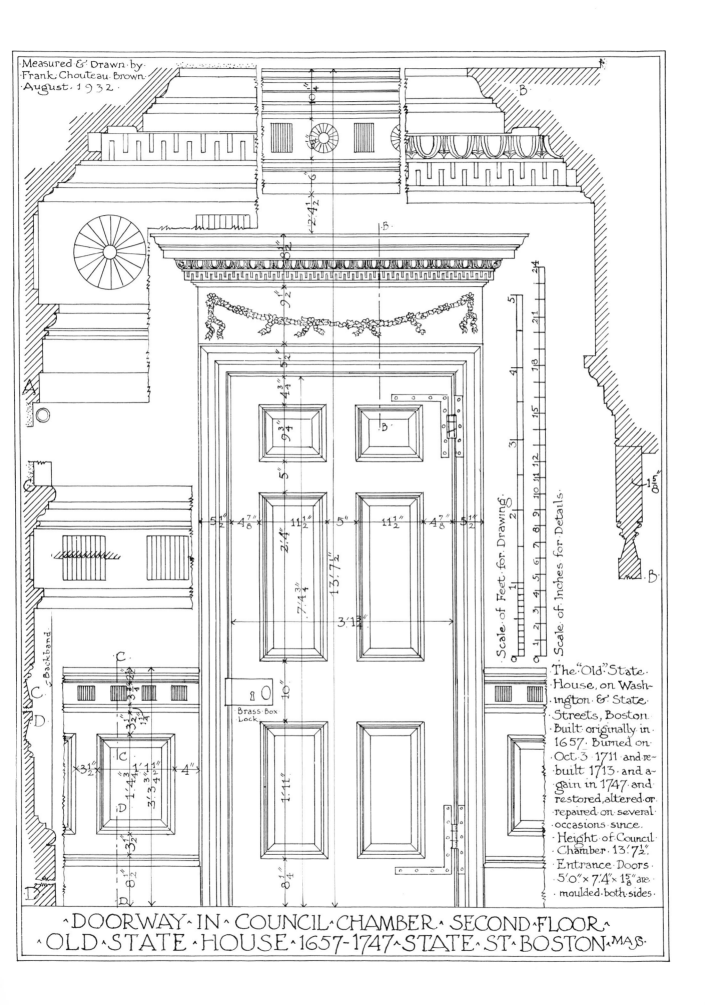

Measured & Drawn by
Frank Chouteau Brown
August 1932

Scale of Feet for Drawing.

Scale of Inches for Details.

Backband

Brass Box Lock

The "Old" State
House, on Wash-
ington & State
Streets, Boston.
Built originally in
1657. Burned on
Oct. 3. 1711. and re-
built 1713. and a-
gain in 1747. and
restored, altered or
repaired on several
occasions since.
Height of Council
Chamber. 13'.7½".
Entrance Doors
5'.0"× 7'.4"× 1⅝" are
moulded both sides.

· DOORWAY · IN · COUNCIL · CHAMBER · SECOND · FLOOR ·
· OLD · STATE · HOUSE · 1657-1747 · STATE · ST · BOSTON · MASS.

Eight Paneled Door

Eight Paneled Door

WARNER HOUSE, PORTSMOUTH, NEW HAMPSHIRE

leather "hinges," or the inter-locked staples or "eyes" that were often found in English cabinets and American chests of a contemporary or earlier time. The rough boarded doors to the two attic entrances of the old West Newbury house are still hung by heavy pieces of leather about 5″ square by a full ¼″ thick—with four nails driven and clinched into door and board adjoining.

Probably the simplest "strap" hinge forms succeeded these two cruder means of hinging or swinging the door; which was still a "battened" affair, usually cut and formed from the featheredged "boarding" that comprised the first type of "paneled" wall treatment. Sometimes the doors were made up of two thicknesses, the upright boarding of one room being nailed against the simple paneled face showing in the one adjoining. This made the use of the cross batten unnecessary, as the boards were held by the framed panels backing them. "H" and "H & L" hinges were soon adopted for light interior paneled doors—which were rarely more than an inch in thickness!—while long strap hinges continued to be employed for heavy, outside, and all unusually wide or boarded doors.

For latches, there was the early wooden latch, with its leather or string to open from the outer side. The simple iron latch, with handle and thumbpiece, probably soon supplanted this; on inner doors, at any rate—though the simple wooden "button," held by a screw, still continued to be sufficient for many years for closet and cupboard doors. Then the small brass latch, cut in, with a ring handle upon both sides, as in the West Newbury house, was found employed in some of the better class dwellings—just as the brass box lock was used in more elegant houses when the iron box lock came into use for simpler habitations; and both, of course, succeeding the earlier wooden, iron bound, box covered lock. And there were also a varied number of "open face" iron latches, some with cast brass knobs or handles, made by colonial smiths for use on inside house doors, in place of the earlier simple iron handle and latch with thumbpiece.

Several types of the earliest door treatments have been included—along with a careful delineation of such original hardware as they still exhibit—not only in order to record the varying manner in which their proportions are kept always appealing and interesting; but also to meet the demand that is increasingly manifest for the most exact and detailed information about work of these more informal and picturesque early American periods. A number of the illustrations have been selected from a little known house at West Newbury, partly because it contains the necessary variety of material, but also from the fortunate fact that much of it is original, while what has been repaired—a process that is as yet only partially carried out—or restored has been done most carefully by the present owner, Mr. J. B. Shearer, under guidance of the architect who has made the accompanying measured drawings, and is therefore thoroughly familiar with the work illustrated.

Several two paneled doors have been portrayed as representative of many examples which exhibit wide variety, particularly in the panel moulding, and the location of the cross stile.

Door to Hall from Drawing Room
LEE MANSION, MARBLEHEAD, MASSACHUSETTS

To include some representation of other than residential doorways, two examples now found in the Old State House, at the head of State Street, in Boston, are employed; although the many vicissitudes and changes through which this historic building has passed make it extremely uncertain as to exactly what period these doors and their surrounding framework may properly be attributed. They will illustrate a somewhat heavier and more "public building" type of treatment, as well as many suggestions of their probable derivation from the finish and records remaining after the several early fires.

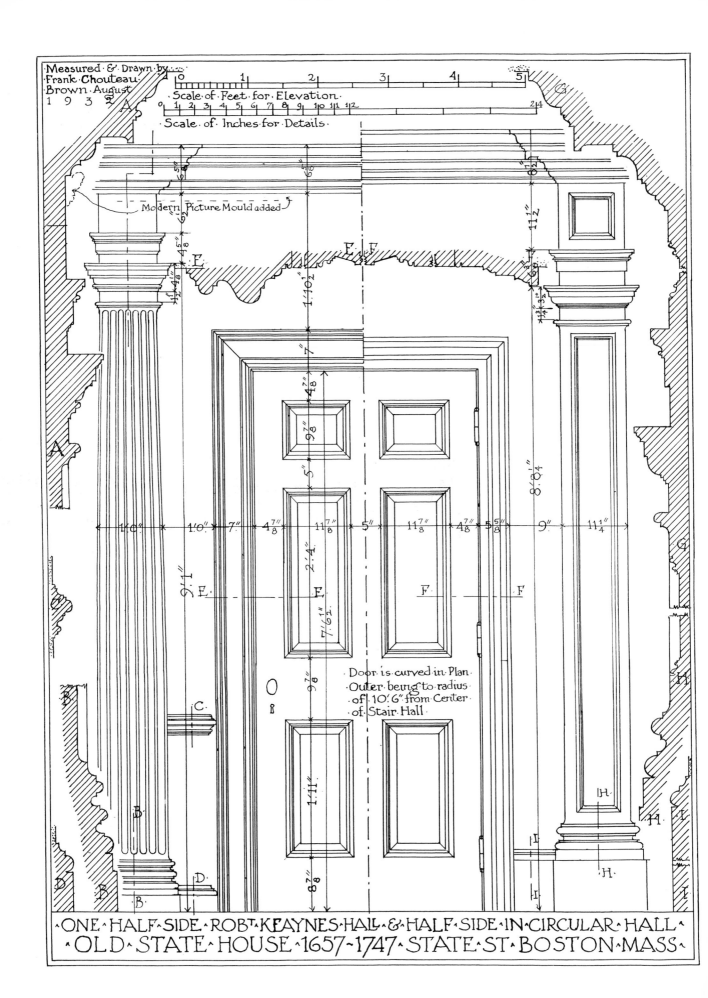

Measured & Drawn by Frank Chouteau Brown August 1932

Scale of Feet for Elevation

Scale of Inches for Details

Modern Picture Mould added

Door is curved in Plan
Outer being to radius
of 10' 6" from Center
of Stair Hall

·ONE·HALF·SIDE·ROBᵀ·KEAYNES·HALL·&·HALF·SIDE·IN·CIRCULAR·HALL·
·OLD·STATE·HOUSE·1657~1747·STATE·ST·BOSTON·MASS·

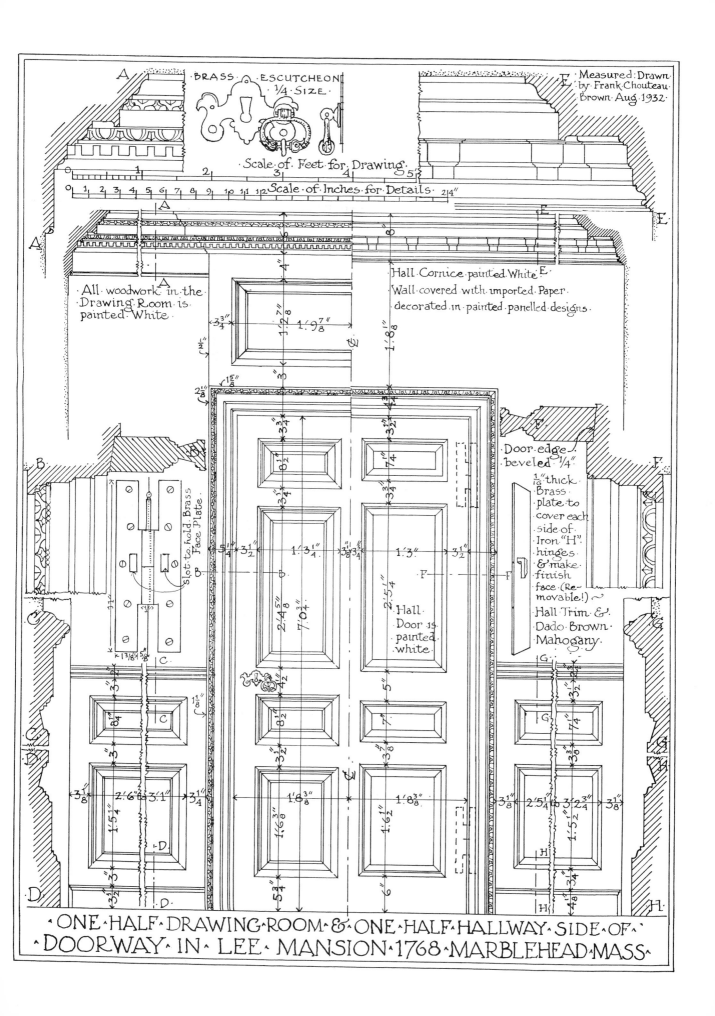

BRASS · ESCUTCHEON
¼ · SIZE ·

Measured · Drawn
by · Frank · Chouteau ·
Brown · Aug · 1932 ·

Scale · of · Feet · for · Drawing ·

Scale · of · Inches · for · Details ·

· All · woodwork · in · the
Drawing · Room · is
painted · White ·

Hall · Cornice · painted · White ·
Wall · covered · with · imported · Paper ·
decorated · in · painted · panelled · designs ·

Slot · to · hold · Brass
Face · Plate ·

Door · edge ·
beveled · ¼" ·

⅛" · thick ·
Brass
plate · to
cover · each ·
side · of ·
Iron · "H" ·
hinges ·
& · make ·
finish ·
face · (Re-
movable!) ~

Hall · Trim · &
Dado · Brown ·
Mahogany ·

Hall ·
Door · is ·
painted ·
white ·

· ONE · HALF · DRAWING · ROOM · & · ONE · HALF · HALLWAY · SIDE · OF ·
· DOORWAY · IN · LEE · MANSION · 1768 · MARBLEHEAD · MASS ·

Six Paneled Door
OLD STATE HOUSE, STATE STREET, BOSTON, MASSACHUSETTS

Six Paneled Door

Entrance Halls and Stairways

Text by
Frank Chouteau Brown
Photographs by
Arthur C. Haskell
Originally published in 1939 as White Pine Monograph
Volume XXV, Number 2

Entrance Hall and Staircase
SARAH ORNE JEWETT HOUSE, SOUTH BERWICK, MAINE
Built by John Haggins in 1774.

ENTRANCE HALLS AND STAIRWAYS ILLUSTRATED BY EXAMPLES FROM MASSACHUSETTS AND CENTRAL NEW ENGLAND

THE entrance hallway was a refinement in living to which most of the early emigrants to the New World had been unaccustomed in their own homeland. Those leaving the south of England had previously been living in survivals from medieval culture, principally in the farmsteads and village cottages, of which many picturesque examples have survived to the present day. Their picturesqueness, however, did not provide even the elemental comforts and conveniences to which every individual believes himself entitled today. Even the smaller manor house plan did not always provide any hall, and when it did it took then the form rather of a general living space than any area intended only for circulation and privacy in connecting the various residential elements of the family menage. In Louis XIV's palace at Versailles, the further bedrooms could only be reached by passing through all those between.

In 1600 the mass of English architecture was of Tudor or earlier date. It was to be a dozen or more years before Inigo Jones returned from Italy, with his 1601 edition of Palladio crowded with his own marginal annotations; and a good many more years were to elapse before the newer style of open plan was to become familiar, even to the wealthier and more sycophantic courtiers of Henry VIII and Elizabeth; and more years still before it began to affect in the slightest the types of common dwellings with which those who first settled the Massachusetts Bay Colony were familiar. Along our southern coast, to be sure, the plans and appearance of the larger houses began much earlier to disclose that they were in some small part expressive of the new fashions in the amenities of living that were permeating the newer and better dwellings of England, especially those of early Georgian date.

Neither did the English climate require much shelter for these cottage dwellers, save from the rain; consequently, the outer entrance door usually opened directly into one end of the general living, eating, and cooking room of the small cottage. It was this one general room that the earliest homes in New England first reproduced, with a large fireplace for cooking and heating. A large scullery opening off this room and another space to provide warm sleeping quarters for the family were the first additions. The space under the roof long remained an undivided attic for the sleeping quarters of children or servants, almost to the present century, and many examples are still to be found in outer New England.

But the rigorous climate of the northern colonies soon forced the settlers to adopt different details of arrangement than they had found livable in the Tudor dwellings of old England. So, to protect the occupants of the hall or fire room from drafts when the entrance door was opened, this was removed behind the corner of the large fireplace (A, page 182), with an inner partition and door to make a "vestibule," out of the other side of which a ladder or steep winding stair—which otherwise might be placed in one corner of the fire room—might rise to the low attic story above. When the house was enlarged by adding another room beyond the fireplace, as at B, page 182 (or in the Haskell House, Volume IX, Chapter 14), we have the typical early "two-room" house plan. A more fully developed entry hall may be seen at C (and on page 198, Volume X, Chapter 12). The very restricted floor area of this entry hall was often later enlarged, generally in the early years of the nineteenth century, by moving the front door and hall wall forward, outside the main wall of the dwelling, as in the Judge Holten House, page 183 (and Volume VII, Chapter 3).

As the houses became more definitely two-story-and-attic structures, the hall and stairway increased in size and importance; a development that became even more definite when the plan increased to four rooms upon each floor. Then such arrangements as at D and

E, page 182 (and page 208, Volume X, Chapter 12) came into general use, but were soon superseded by the more spacious types F and G, page 182, and the decorative forms that they assume in the photographs on other pages in this chapter. Among the earlier examples of plan D, is the Joseph Peaslee Hall at Rock Village, 1675 (page 200, Volume X, Chapter 12); from which simplicity an advance was shortly made to some of the more spacious and pretentious treatments shown in this chapter.

The staircase now had usually two instead of the earlier three runs, and the first was made much the longer, in order to obtain headroom, usually for passage purposes to other parts of the house plan, under the cross landing or last run at the rear end of the open hall. Among the most dignified of these presentations was the entrance hall with under-arch, and main cross landing with its Palladian window-door opening at that level onto the rear staircase, which was the one that then continued to the third story, leaving the main staircase to end

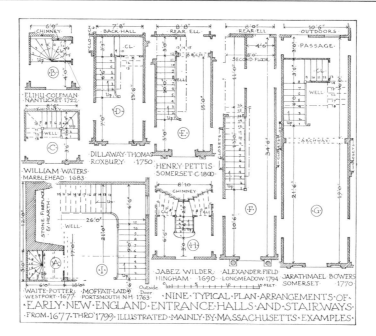

NINE·TYPICAL·PLAN·ARRANGEMENTS·OF·
EARLY·NEW·ENGLAND·ENTRANCE·HALLS·AND·STAIRWAYS·
·FROM·1677·THRO'1799·ILLUSTRATED·MAINLY·BY·MASSACHUSETTS·EXAMPLES·

Courtesy Halliday Historic Collection

Entrance Hall, Archway, and Staircase
COL. ISAAC ROYALL HOUSE — c1733 — MEDFORD

upon the second story level and so connect only with the principal front second story rooms. A fine example of this arrangement was in the Benjamin Hall, Jr., House, at Medford: one of three Hall family houses existing since 1785, side by side, until the summer of 1938, when this particular building succumbed to commercial pressure and was unfortunately demolished (page 182)!

That varied decorative treatments of this landing doorway connecting the front and rear halls were frequently found in Massachusetts, is indicated by the two other examples, both from Salem, that appear side by side on page 187. Of course, this is merely another expression of the graceful and impressive arched window motive, that often appears in the rear house wall, to open on the main staircase hall landing, as in the Jeremiah Lee Mansion, 1768, in Marblehead (pages 196 and 204, Volume X, Chapter 12), and elsewhere.

With the fully-developed two-room-deep long entrance hallway, G, page 182, a large archway

Side View of Entrance Vestibule
JUDGE SAMUEL HOLTEN HOUSE — 1670 — DANVERS, MASSACHUSETTS

Courtesy Soc. Pres. N. E. Antiquities

Entrance Hall, Showing Crossbeam and Staircase
TOBIAS LEAR HOUSE — c1740 — PORTSMOUTH, NEW HAMPSHIRE

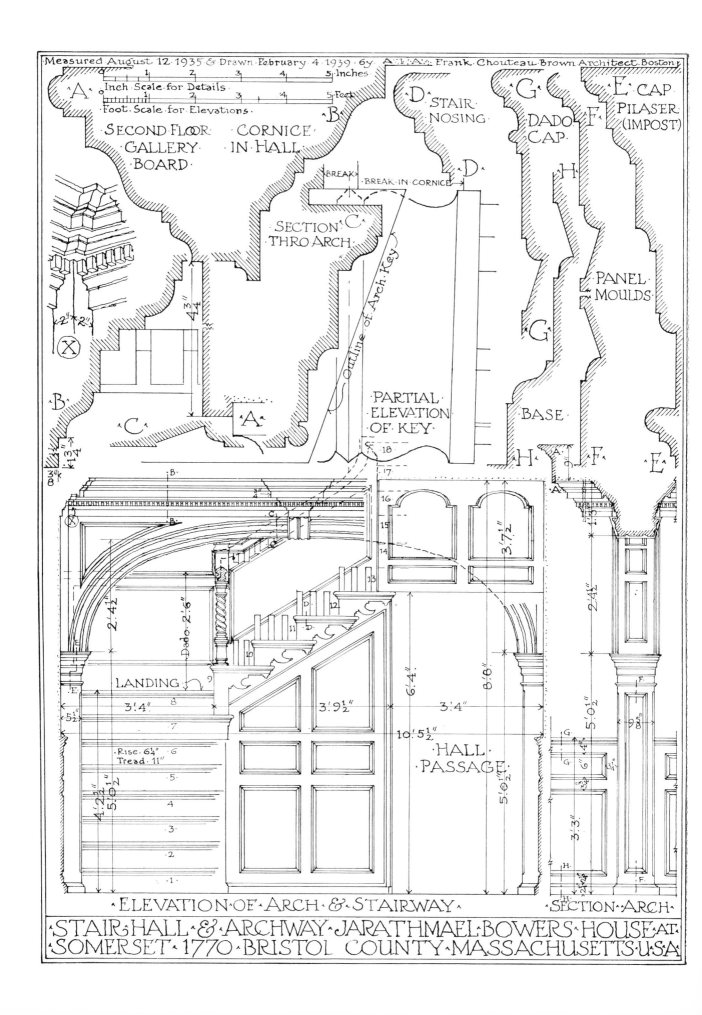

Measured August 12 1935 & Drawn February 4 1939 by A.I.A. Frank Chouteau Brown Architect Boston

Inch Scale for Details
Foot Scale for Elevations.

A SECOND FLOOR GALLERY BOARD

CORNICE IN HALL

B

D STAIR NOSING

G G DADO CAP

E CAP PILASER (IMPOST)

F

H

PANEL MOULDS

BREAK
BREAK IN CORNICE
D

SECTION C THRO ARCH

Outline of Arch Key

PARTIAL ELEVATION OF KEY

BASE

B

C

A

X

2" 2"

4 3/4"

3 1/4"

3/8"

H A F E

ELEVATION OF ARCH & STAIRWAY

SECTION ARCH

LANDING

3'4"

Rise 6 1/4"
Tread 11"

Dado 2'6"

2'4 1/2"

5 1/2"

4'2 1/2"
5'0 1/2"

HALL PASSAGE

3'9 1/2"

6'4"

3'4"

8'6"

10'5 1/2"

5'0 1/2"

3'7 1/2"

2'4 1/2"

5'0 1/2"

9 1/2"

6'4"

3'3"

G G

H

F

·STAIR·HALL·&·ARCHWAY·JARATHMAEL·BOWERS·HOUSE·AT·
·SOMERSET·1770·BRISTOL·COUNTY·MASSACHUSETTS·USA·

crossing the hall near the center of its length, and recessing the staircase within a further hallway, makes its appearance. In its earliest form, it may be seen as a simple exposed structural girder, crossing the ceiling of the hall at this location, in the Tobias Lear House, c1740, at Portsmouth, N.H. This is its simplest manifestation. In the region round about Portsmouth there are at least a dozen varied examples of the large hall cross-archway, with a few others in

Vassall, in 1746, to the earlier house, built before 1686, by John Vassall in Cambridge (Volume VII, Chapter 9), with its individual use of an outlined bracket form, in place of a capital, over a very flat wall pilaster from above which the elliptical arch springs; and the somewhat similar arrangement in the entrance hallway of the Col. Isaac Royall House, c1733, at Medford, where the bracket is more elaborate and the pilaster is given a bolder projection.

Courtesy His. Am. Bldgs. Survey

View Through Entrance Hall Archway Toward Staircase
JARATHMAEL BOWERS HOUSE—1770—SOMERSET, MASSACHUSETTS

Maine, in Massachusetts, and also in Rhode Island.

Accompanying examples are the Jewett House, 1774, in South Berwick, Me.; the Bowers House, 1770, in Somerset; the Captain Gregory Purcell (John Paul Jones) House, 1757-1759, in Portsmouth, N.H.; and the Nickels-Sortwell House, 1807-1808, in Wiscasset, Maine. Two other examples near Boston are the cross-hall arch in the portion added by Maj. Henry

A radically different and unusual plan is shown at H, page 182, from the Jabez Wilder Cottage, at Hingham, 1690. Here the staircase starts upward from just inside the entrance door and in the middle of the hallway, with a flight which divides and rises at right and left against the receding face of the chimney, to end at the very doorways of the two rooms under its "rainbow" roof. Finally, at I, page 182, is the plan

Palladian Door-Window to Rear Hall on Landing

First Story Hall, Under-Arch, and Stair

BENJAMIN HALL, JR., HOUSE—1785—MEDFORD, MASSACHUSETTS

Doorway to Rear Hall, Intermediate Landing
ASSEMBLY HOUSE—1782—SALEM, MASSACHUSETTS

Doorway to Rear Hall, First Landing
JOSHUA WARD HOUSE—c1765—SALEM, MASSACHUSETTS

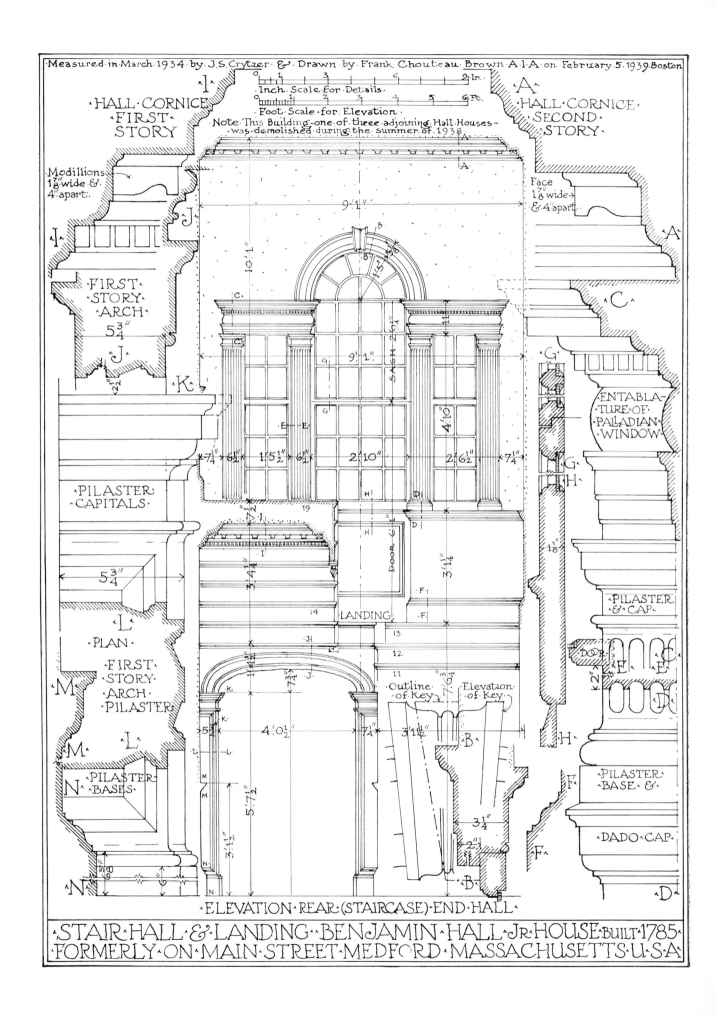

Measured in March 1934 by J.S. Crytzer & Drawn by Frank Chouteau Brown A.I.A on February 5.1939. Boston

· Inch · Scale · for · Details ·

· Foot · Scale · for · Elevation ·

Note. This Building one of three adjoining Hall Houses was demolished during the summer of 1938.

·HALL·CORNICE·
·FIRST·
·STORY·

·HALL·CORNICE·
·SECOND·
·STORY·

Modillions 1⅞" wide & 4" apart.

Face 1⅞" wide & 4" apart.

·FIRST·STORY·ARCH· 5¾"

·ENTABLA-TURE·OF·PALADIAN·WINDOW·

·PILASTER·CAPITALS·

·PLAN·FIRST·STORY·ARCH·PILASTER·

·PILASTER·& ·CAP·

·PILASTER·BASES·

·LANDING·

·Outline of Key·   ·Elevation of Key·

·PILASTER·BASE·&·

·DADO·CAP·

·ELEVATION·REAR·(STAIRCASE)·END·HALL·

·STAIR·HALL·&·LANDING·BENJAMIN·HALL·JR·HOUSE·BUILT·1785·
·FORMERLY·ON·MAIN·STREET·MEDFORD·MASSACHUSETTS·U·S·A·

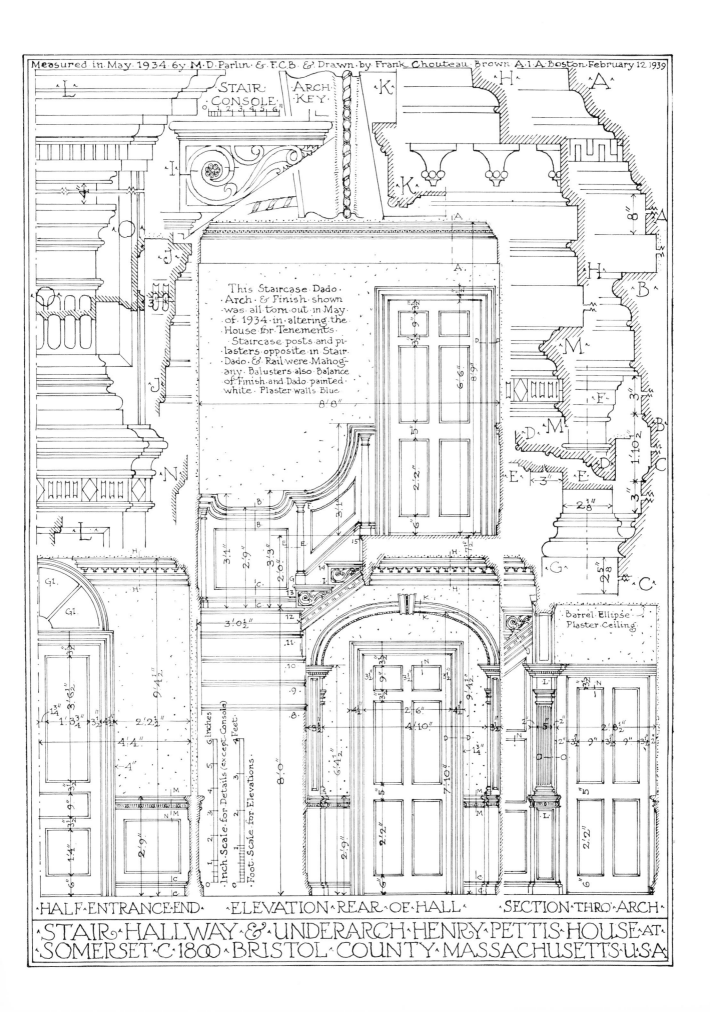

STAIR CONSOLE

ARCH KEY

This Staircase·Dado·
·Arch·&·Finish·shown·
was·all·torn·out·in·May·
of·1934·in·altering·the·
House·for·Tenements·
Staircase·posts·and·pi-
lasters·opposite·in·Stair·
Dado·&·Rail·were·Mahog-
any·Balusters·also·Balance·
of·Finish·and·Dado·painted·
white·Plaster·walls·Blue

Barrel·Ellipse·
Plaster·Ceiling

Inch·Scale·for·Details·(except·Console)

Foot·Scale·for·Elevations·

·HALF·ENTRANCE·END·   ·ELEVATION·REAR·OF·HALL·   ·SECTION·THRO·ARCH·

STAIR·HALLWAY·&·UNDERARCH·HENRY·PETTIS·HOUSE·AT·
·SOMERSET·C·1800·BRISTOL·COUNTY·MASSACHUSETTS·U·S·A·

from "Colonial Architecture in New England"

Entrance Hall and Staircase
MOFFATT-LADD HOUSE—1763—PORTSMOUTH, NEW HAMPSHIRE

Hallway Looking Toward Front Entrance
COLEMAN-HOLLISTER HOUSE—1796—GREENFIELD, MASSACHUSETTS

Semicircular Staircase in Recess off Entrance Hall
COLEMAN-HOLLISTER HOUSE — 1796 — GREENFIELD, MASSACHUSETTS
Asher Benjamin, Architect

Entrance Hall, Looking Toward Front Door
NICKELS-SORTWELL HOUSE — 1807–1808 — WISCASSET, MAINE

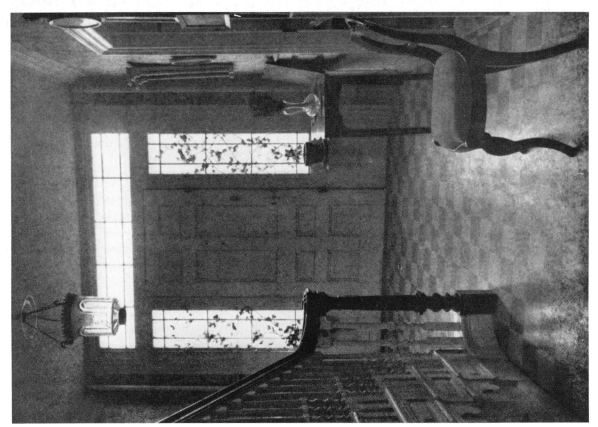

Entrance Hall, Looking Toward Front Door
AZOR ORNE HOUSE — c1765 — MARBLEHEAD, MASS.

of a quite unusual *corner* entrance hall, as it appears in the Moffatt-Ladd House, 1763, at Portsmouth, N.H. The same plan is repeated, upon a somewhat smaller scale, in at least two other Portsmouth houses.

Despite the apparently elaborate layout of several of these hall plans, all (with the possible exception of the one last named) nevertheless conform within a reasonably economical floor area, in relation to the space covered by the whole house. In the case of the

toward each other, to meet on a short landing near the center of the hall's length, with a final short run of two or three steps at right angle, to the floor above.

Although this chapter is given to the entrance hall, rather than the staircase; yet the two are so closely associated in early New England house plans, that it is not possible to picture one without the other. That much more might be made of the hall-way is proven by the Azor Orne and Nickels-Sortwell

Courtesy Soc. Pres. N. E. Antiquities

Entrance Hall, Archway, and Staircase
CAPTAIN GREGORY PURCELL HOUSE — 1757-1759 — PORTSMOUTH, NEW HAMPSHIRE

Nickels-Sortwell Hall, the effect of entrance hallway, cross arch, and staircase are all secured within the one-room house depth, as appears more plainly, perhaps, by referring to other illustrations of this hall, in Volume VII, Chapter 12.

Finally, mention should be made of another arrangement of staircases, each starting from near the doors at front and back house walls, and running

entrances; while in the Coleman-Hollister hallway, no staircase appears until the center of the hall is passed, when this charmingly delicate stairway comes into full view. With the exception of this example, and the stairway of the Nickels-Sortwell House, the elliptical or semicircular stair plan — usually a later and more sophisticated development — is not presented in this chapter.

Hall and Archway, Looking Toward Garden Door
MERRIMAN HOUSE — c1820 — BRISTOL, RHODE ISLAND

View Along Entrance Hall Toward Rear Door
SQUIRE WILLIAM SEVER HOUSE — 1760 — KINGSTON, MASS.

New England Staircases

Text by
Benjamin Graham
Photographs by
Arthur C. Haskell
Originally published in 1933 as White Pine Monograph
Volume XIX, Number 5

Stair Hall
LEE MANSION, MARBLEHEAD, MASSACHUSETTS

SOME NEW ENGLAND STAIRCASES—1670–1770

WHEN the first colonial dwellings began to attain the dignity of a full second story, with rooms of useable height, the temporary ladder-like arrangement that had previously served to reach the upper floor changed to a more permanent and a more ornamental feature in the American home. Sometimes it ran directly between partitions of wide board sheathing or plaster or, starting with a quarter wind at the bottom, it went steeply upward to the low chambers overhead. Or it reversed this process, starting straight up from beside the kitchen in the "linter" (or lean-to), attaining the floor above with a quarter turn to right or left, as the case might be.

When the location against the front of a large chimney serving two end rooms, and possibly also a third at the rear, became common, the latter stair plan was soon changed to a flight of three runs—as in the Waters House at Marblehead—with either landings or winders at the corner angles, depending upon the height to be gained and the width of the chimney itself. Usually the chimney was spacious enough to permit of the landing (as in the Salmon Falls staircase), thus making the stairs easier to take by means of the brief "breather" at the turn, breaking up the steepness of the runs, generally of three to five risers each. And this remained the favorite stair arrangement, until the chimneys were removed to the outer end walls or placed midway between a pair of end

rooms, when the hall might be run entirely through the house from front to back, with a long straight flight of stairs, sometimes with a turn at top or bottom.

The staircase of the old-time New England house is always one of its most attractive adjuncts. No matter how simple, its proportions are almost invariably good and it is generally regarded as a most attractive feature of the early colonial structure. Even the crudest and most primitive examples are today accepted as interesting exhibits of the inherent feeling of their builders for the design appropriate to its environment and the method of construction that was most perfectly adapted to express the materials available.

In the earliest existing houses, where the stairs are still to be seen in something approaching their original condition, built perhaps during the last half of the seventeenth century, the staircases usually had no baluster of any kind. It was then customary to extend the simple boarded face of the partition under the stair run up to the height of a low rail or to the level of the second story floor above, thus stiffening the stair construction and simplifying the problem of protecting the stair edge.

When the boarding—usually at that time some variation of the featheredge pattern—did not extend up to the second floor timbering, it sometimes stopped at a height of two feet to thirty inches above the step rise, and was capped with a narrow moulded crown strip, with a small bed-moulding upon the face, or upon both sides. Or it might merely extend from the first floor to the stair stringer and a single piece of hand railing carried between simple rough posts at top and bottom, with the space below left open—as was probably the original condition of the Dr. Peaslee stairway in the brick garrison house at Rock Village, Massachusetts, dating from 1675.

Of course, at that time, the entire stair construction was suspended from two "buttresses" or "raised stringers," one on each side of the steps, into which the risers and treads were housed. These supports were usually about 10 by 2 inches, and there were no intermediate stringers used between, as supports, as is the modern custom. Often this stairway was left in its open and unadorned simplicity, as in the example from the Dennison House (shown in Vol. III, Chapter 14) at Annisquam; where the work was carried out in pine, fashioned after the earlier oak staircases, of which there are several examples dating from about 1675. Again, with this form of design, and either one or two sloping rails pinned at each end into the upright posts at landing and floor levels, this treatment served as a sort of structural truss, obviously stiffening the carriage of the stairs, and suspending each flight from end to end, even with a turn or landing in between.

Most early staircases were so cramped that they were perforce carried around angles in the plan with a series of steps, making what is known as a wind, rather than the pleasanter and easier landing—as in the King Hooper, Waters, rear Warner stairs, and other numerous examples. And the angles of these winding steps are very generally not at the usual 22½, 30 or 45 degree, so regularly employed in modern stairbuilding, but some slight variation of these angles, the stair winders being usually worked or handled around the post, in the manner that appears in the plan of the Dennison staircase, and others here indicated.

Another detail characteristic of the early staircases is the informal variance of the height of the rail above tread and gallery level, being often higher than is the modern custom and, occasionally, much lower, while in those instances (as in the Wentworth Mansion at Salmon Falls) where the rail on each run of the flight is a handworked ramp made in one piece of material, it shows considerable extremes of height, as appears in the varied lengths of the balusters.

The old rule-of-thumb proportioning of stair-rise to stair-tread dimension—"that twice the rise added to the width of tread should equal 25 inches" (or, at least, come within the extremes of 24 to 26 inches)—has been pretty consistently adhered to in all old work.

The turned baluster was probably introduced some time between 1675 and 1700. At first wide-spaced and roughly turned or "whittled" out of soft wood (as in the Peaslee stairs at Rock Village) it was often—as there—inserted under older existing rails. Its turnings gradually became more ornate and elaborate—

as in the Salmon Falls Mansion House, where a baluster pattern very advanced and delicate for its period, with an informal irregularity of turning that naively bespeaks its probable original date—until we reach the perfections obtained in the fine mahogany and workmanship of the spacious front stairs of the famed Jeremiah Lee Mansion at Marblehead, with its majestic width of seven feet!

It seems impossible that this fine workmanship was achieved by the inventive artisan, from a simple turning lathe. Yet the elaborate and delicately moulded posts and balusters of the Lee Mansion must have been achieved in 1768 with a common lathe, foot or water-powered. With this simple implement, geared to a slow even turning, a skilled workman could mark out these twists and spirals with the edge of his chisel, grooving them as deeply as he dared: and then, with their regularity once established, he could complete the grooving by hand, and finish off the twist at top or bottom by carving—as was always necessary, even with the most improved machines for this work, of which the earliest known in New England was not developed before 1860 and 1865.

Or notice the skill and perfection of thoroughness with which the Dillaway House stairway has been worked out. This perfection may be contrasted with the Short House stairs, done in the advanced, comparatively rich and populous settlement of Newbury, and made for a far wealthier man than the simple parson who built the Dillaway House across the street from his church on Eliot Square in Roxbury. For the Short House balusters, as magnified in their shadows on the wall, betray almost the extremes of variation, in their turnings and patterns, of any of the examples illustrated in this collection.

Some of these same variations are to be found in the earlier named Warner House at Portsmouth, built between 1718 and 1722, at a cost of 10,000 pounds by one Capt. McPhedris. But here probably other elements must be taken into account. Only the rear staircase now seems plausibly harmonious with its period. The front flight has been subjected to extensive alterations; probably the closed-in type of gallery treatment found on the landing and second floor expressing the older—and perhaps the original—design. The workmanship along the runs, and stair ends, dating from some later rebuilding or change—even though made soon after the dwelling was completed!

The Lee Mansion front stairs, with double twisted newel, three differently designed balusters on each tread, and its mahogany rail ramped at the stair well angles as well as at the landings, is among the most elaborate stair designs of the period. It also shows the characteristic wall dado, its cap following out the ramps and eases of the stair rail, but at a height some ten inches above the latter, that appears in all the best examples. Finally it also exhibits the boxed-in undercarriage, paneled upon the back face, that shows under the second run, extending from the landing to the second floor level.

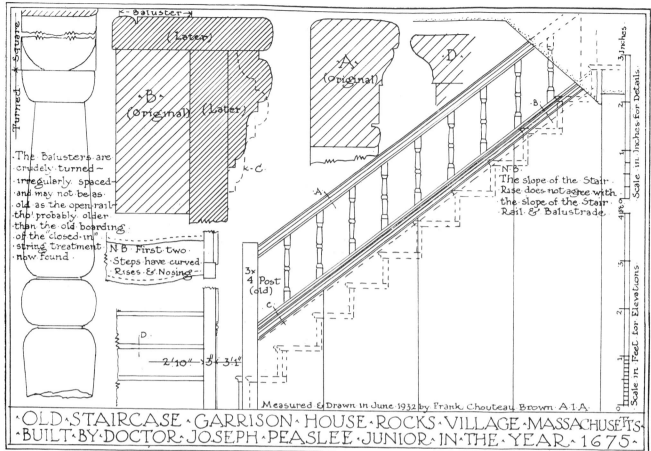

·OLD·STAIRCASE·GARRISON·HOUSE·ROCKS·VILLAGE·MASSACHVSETTS·
·BVILT·BY·DOCTOR·JOSEPH·PEASLEE·JVNIOR·IN·THE·YEAR·1675·

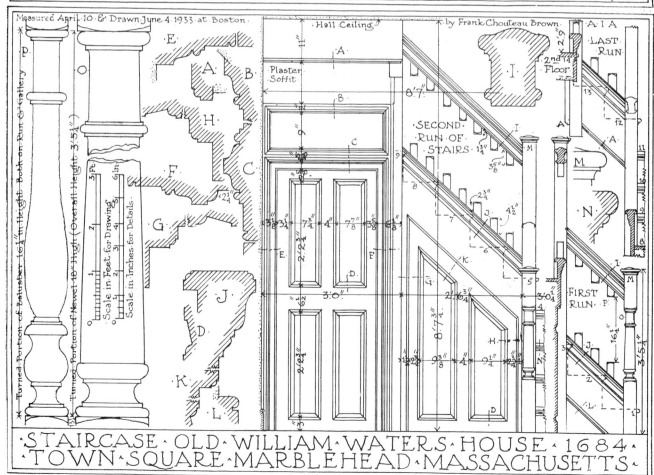

·STAIRCASE·OLD·WILLIAM·WATERS·HOUSE·1684·
·TOWN·SQVARE·MARBLEHEAD·MASSACHVSETTS·

JOSEPH PEASLEE STAIRCASE —1675—ROCK VILLAGE, MASS.
Measured drawings shown on page 199.

WILLIAM WATERS STAIRCASE —1684— MARBLEHEAD, MASS.

WARNER HOUSE STAIRCASE—1718-1722—PORTSMOUTH, N.H.
Measured drawing on page 203.

PAUL WENTWORTH STAIRCASE—1701—SALMON FALLS, N.H.
Measured drawing on page 202.

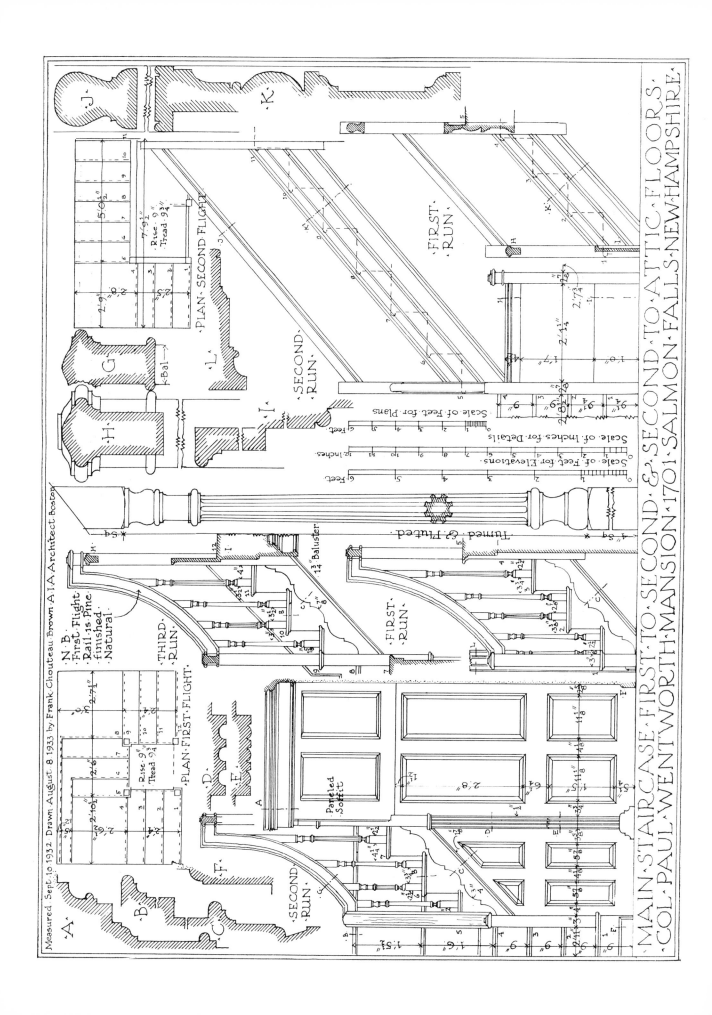

MAIN·STAIRCASE·FIRST·TO·SECOND·&·SECOND·TO·ATTIC·FLOORS·
·COL·PAUL·WENTWORTH·MANSION·1701·SALMON·FALLS·NEW·HAMPSHIRE·

Measured· Sept.10.1932· Drawn· August. 8.1933 by Frank·Chouteau·Brown·A·I·A· Architect· Boston·

·J· ·K·

·FIRST· ·RUN·

·PLAN· SECOND· FLIGHT·

·SECOND· ·RUN·

Rise· 9"
Tread· 9¼"
7'-9½"
5'-0½"

·G· ·L·
·H· ·I·

Scale of Feet for Plans
Scale of Inches for Details
Scale of Feet for Elevations

·THIRD· ·RUN·

·FIRST· ·RUN·

N·B·
First· Flight·
Rail· is· Pine·
finished·
Natural·

13" Baluster

Turned & Fluted

·PLAN· FIRST· FLIGHT·

Rise· 9"
Tread· 9¼"

·A· ·B· ·C· ·D· ·E· ·F·

Paneled
Soffit

·SECOND· ·RUN·

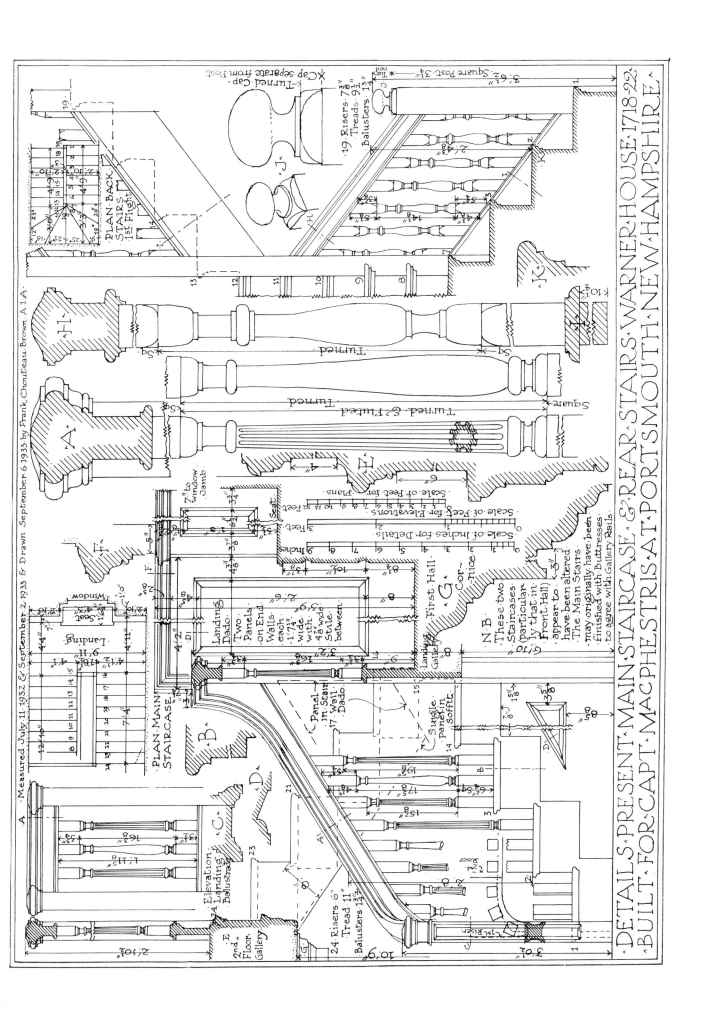

DETAILS·PRESENT·MAIN·STAIRCASE·&·REAR·STAIRS·WARNER·HOUSE·1718-22·
·BUILT·FOR·CAPT·MACPHESTRIS·AT·PORTSMOUTH·NEW·HAMPSHIRE·

Measured August 12 & Drawn August 18 1933 by Frank Chouteau Brown A.I.A

·WEST·WINDOW·&·WALL·ON·STAIRCASE·LANDING·
·JEREMIAH·LEE·MANSION·1768·MARBLEHEAD·MASS·

JEREMIAH LEE MANSION—1768—MARBLEHEAD, MASSACHUSETTS
Measured drawings shown on pages 204, 206, and 207.

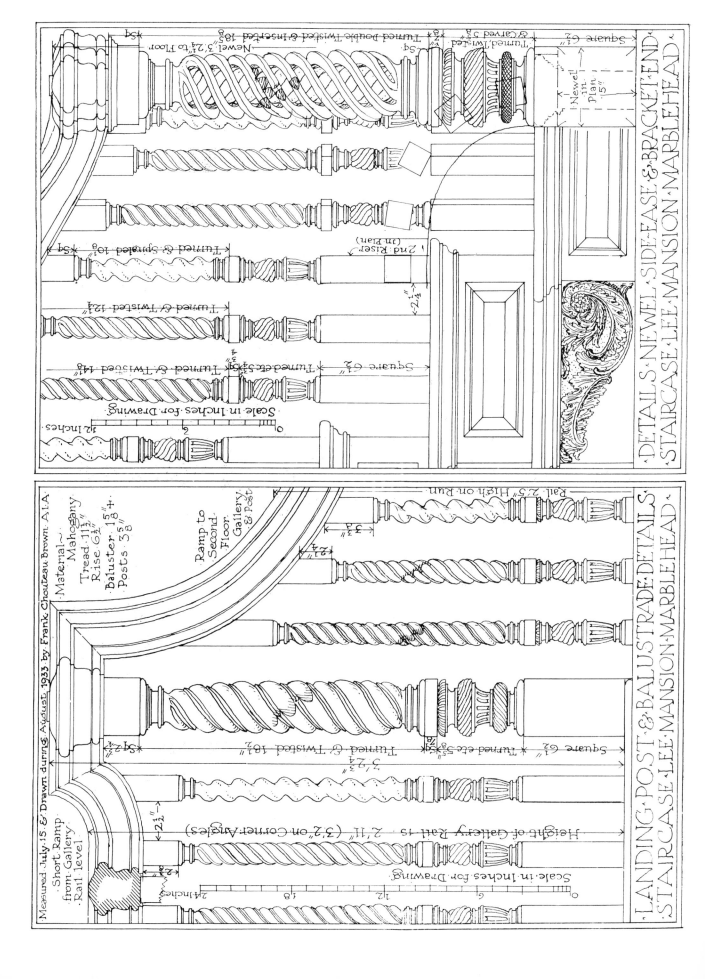

·DETAILS·NEWEL·SIDE·EASE·&·BRACKET·END·
·STAIRCASE·LEE·MANSION·MARBLEHEAD·

·LANDING·POST·&·BALUSTRADE·DETAILS·
·STAIRCASE·LEE·MANSION·MARBLEHEAD·

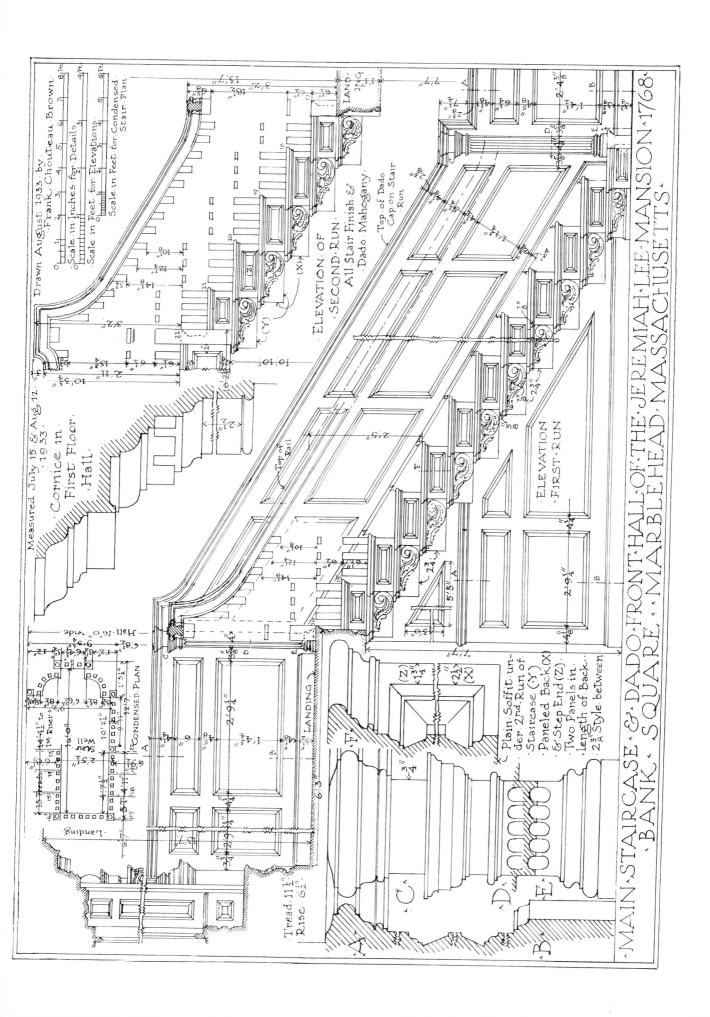

·MAIN·STAIRCASE·&·DADO·FRONT·HALL·OF·THE·JEREMIAH·LEE·MANSION·1768·
·BANK·SQUARE·MARBLEHEAD·MASSACHUSETTS·

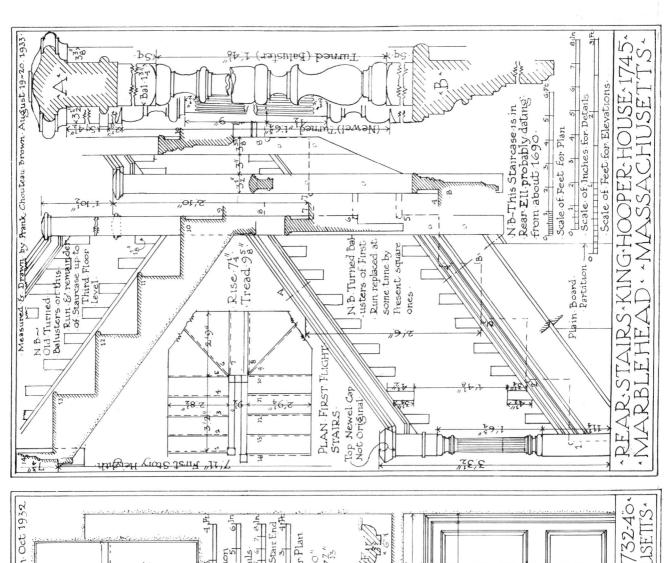

REAR·STAIRS·KING·HOOPER·HOUSE·1745·
·MARBLEHEAD·MASSACHUSETTS·

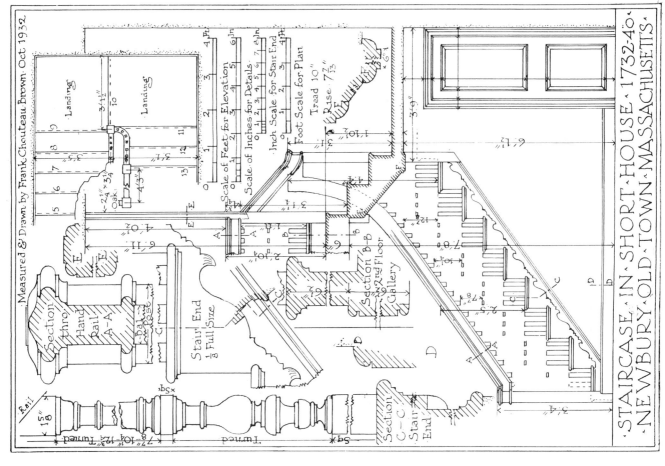

·STAIRCASE·IN·SHORT·HOUSE·1732-40·
·NEWBURY·OLD·TOWN·MASSACHUSETTS·

KING HOOPER REAR STAIRS—1745—MARBLEHEAD, MASS.

SHORT STAIRCASE—1732–1740—NEWBURY OLD TOWN, MASS.

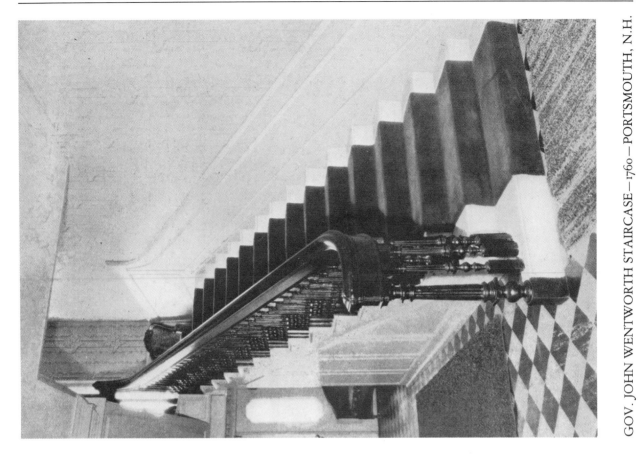

GOV. JOHN WENTWORTH STAIRCASE—1760—PORTSMOUTH, N.H.

DILLAWAY STAIRCASE—1750-1752—ROXBURY, MASS.

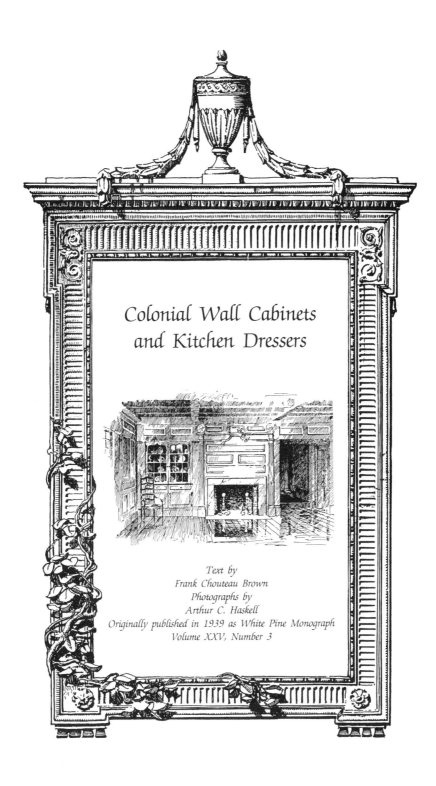

Colonial Wall Cabinets
and Kitchen Dressers

Text by
Frank Chouteau Brown
Photographs by
Arthur C. Haskell
Originally published in 1939 as White Pine Monograph
Volume XXV, Number 3

Wall Cupboard Beside Fireplace in Living Room
EBENEZER WATERS HOUSE — 1767 — WEST SUTTON, MASSACHUSETTS

SOME COLONIAL WALL CABINETS
AND KITCHEN DRESSERS

DURING those first few years, when the tide of passage from England to the Massachusetts Bay settlements was running most strongly space was at a premium in the vessels of diminutive tonnage that were available for the transportation of settlers and their belongings, on the two or three months' journey across the stormy Atlantic. Aside from their most necessary personal belongings, the settlers had to choose between essentials; those items most necessary for the first year's subsistence, at the very least. There was not much space available for livestock and furniture, and yet the former was needed for the permanent settlement of any farming community.

First were the fundamentals: farming tools, at least their metal parts, to which handles could be fitted after arrival; firearms; kitchen utensils, along with powder, shot, fishlines, knives; and a supply of clothing, or the woven material from which it easily could be fashioned. There were also the tools of the various trades—for the carpenter, blacksmith, the miller—not to forget the utensils, spinning and carding, hand looms, etc., needed by the women workers of the colony. Also cooking dishes, pots and pans, and a few precious pieces of furniture. Seeds for the first planting, shoots of fruit trees and shrubs, and the plants and simples for sickness, must not be forgotten.

Fortunately, in the primitive living conditions of that time in England, furniture was a much simpler and more homemade factor in the family life than it is today. And for a journey such as this, with cubical space lacking, only the most prized heirlooms could be transported to the new continent. The family bible, and bible box; an arm chair or two; perhaps a cherished bedstead or table; and an oak dresser might suffice. Chests were, of course, the most widely used and easily transportable of all objects. Every family had more than one of these. Of oak or deal, sturdily framed, they could be stuffed with smaller possessions —cloth, linen, clothing, and other minor personal be-

longings. And at the journey's end, they would go against the wall or under the window, and serve both as a seat and container for clothing, sometimes as a child's bed, until time had been found for the building of other and ampler furniture for the homestead.

The few bedrooms could be furnished sufficiently with a bed, a chair, and a couple of stools, and probably one or more chests, usually one being raised with an additional drawer or two beneath, to make a sort of primitive "bureau." The dining needs were met by a long table, or a short one with drop leaves, a chair or two, some stools or a couple of benches, and perhaps another raised chest, to keep the linen and serve as a sort of sideboard. For the kitchen, the same or another table, a dresser of shelves and cupboards, along with a storage entry or buttery, were all that could be desired. The same room at first served all the family purposes of general living—as kitchen, dining and sitting room, and, often, sleeping room.

The early New England houses provided little space for "closets" within their spare and rigid outlines. But as the settlers' families grew and prospered, as newer and larger houses were built, a considerable ingenuity was employed in providing extra spaces for storage. And, of course, there was always the attic! But in these early dwellings, the attic space was as much used and crowded as all the rest of the house. It was the dormitory for the children, and, a little later, for the slaves or indentured help. It was to be an hundred and more years, at least, before this highly-prized and useful space could deteriorate to become the catch-all and store-all of family *incunabula* that it has been for the last few generations of the fast vanishing breed of American house-dwellers!

In the more informal cottage homes, along the sea coast or in farming communities, there was great use for "cubby-holes" of all sorts, especially in the most used rooms of these dwellings. This would naturally trend toward the filling of all possible recesses with

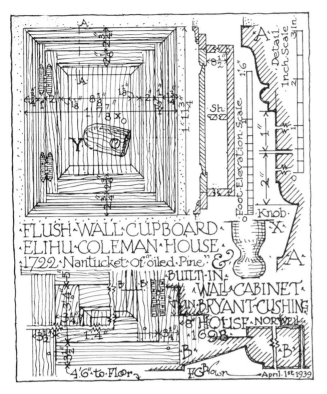

shelves, whether open or covered, in the kitchens and living rooms of the house. And, of course, the recession of the chimney stack from its larger base under the first floor level, to the smaller area above the second floor, would provide opportunity for useful cabinets and cupboards over and around the fireplaces, with their ovens, etc., housed within these chimney bases. In several cases the illustrations show the lower shelf of several cupboard recesses resting directly upon the oak fireplace lintel, which was usually ten to twelve inches thick.

In the Rhode Island section, as in western Massachusetts, these examples are usually found in the simpler cottages and farmhouses. Instances were published in Vol. VI, Chap. 6, all from Little Compton, the Amasa Gray House, William Pabodie (Betty Alden) House, 1682, and the Oliver Almy Place, 1745. A more pretentious and formal example was formerly in the parlor of the Amanda Greene House in Newport. A little further north, in Massachusetts, near Fall River, an unusual and early instance might formerly have been seen in the old Barnaby House, built in Freetown sometime before 1740, and allowed

Fireplace in Old Kitchen with Recesses Over
BARNABY HOUSE — c1740 — FREETOWN, MASSACHUSETTS

Fireplace and Wall Cabinet in Living Room
ELIHU COLEMAN HOUSE — 1722 — NANTUCKET, MASSACHUSETTS

Fireplace and Wall Cabinet in Northwest Room
BRYANT-CUSHING HOUSE — 1698 — NORWELL, MASSACHUSETTS

to fall into disrepair until, in 1936, it finally burned down.

In most houses, whether early or late in date, there seemed to be a very general custom of locating these small wall cupboards, or one of them, over the top of the domed oven, which was usually placed at one side or the other of the large kitchen fireplace. And the resulting small wall cabinet does not always, nor even often, open from the kitchen side of the chimney breast, but appears even more customarily to have the access door in the corner of one of two front rooms of the dwelling (pages 215 and 225). A great many examples of this location are found in old houses, a few of which are shown among those here reproduced. Indeed, in the larger and more important houses, this location seems to be the more prevalent. The obvious use of such a small receptacle would be for church-warden pipes, tobacco, rum or gin, or some of the other ingredients required in the hospitality of the time, for hot toddies, mulled wine, etc. The church-wardens were often exposed in wall racks; but gin, bitters or homemade wines, would probably be kept less conspicuously, by any careful housekeeper; then, as well as now!

There was also use for a small closet cabinet, separately made, and planned so that it could either be attached to the face of

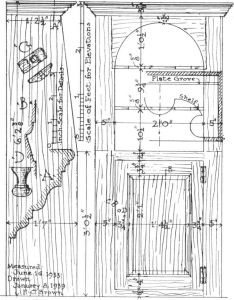

·OLD·WALL·CUPBOARD·ROCKPORT·M&S·

Mantel with Cupboards Over Fireplace in Parlor
AMANDA GREENE HOUSE, NEWPORT, RHODE ISLAND

the boarded wall in some convenient corner of a used room (page 224), or placed out of the way behind some door. And the same sort of cabinet could equally well be set atop any tall desk, chest of drawers, or other piece of furniture, to enlarge its capacity, when backed against a room wall.

Most casual students of colonial buildings seem to expect that their elevations and plans will be developed uniformly, so as to exactly balance upon each side of a center or axial line. As a matter of fact, while often true of late work (and more especially of post-Revolutionary, or Georgian buildings) it is rather the exception than the rule with those of earlier date. Even in the stately dwellings of Virginia and Maryland, a considerable amount of *un*balance exists in most room interiors, generally adding to their interest and charm. In the early, and less formalized, structures of New England, a remarkable amount of pliability is found. Very generally the mantel—supposedly centered in the principal wall, with its attendant features—actually occurs well off the room center.

In this chapter, for instance, the majority of examples show the fireplace wall as an *un*balanced composition. Running through these pages one must believe the colonial builders were little concerned with any

Wall Cabinet with Paneled Doors, Upstairs Sitting Room
CURTIS TAVERN—1765—GRANVILLE, MASSACHUSETTS

Fireplace and Wall Cupboard, Southeast Sitting Room
FEARING-WARR HOUSE—1765—WAREHAM, MASSACHUSETTS

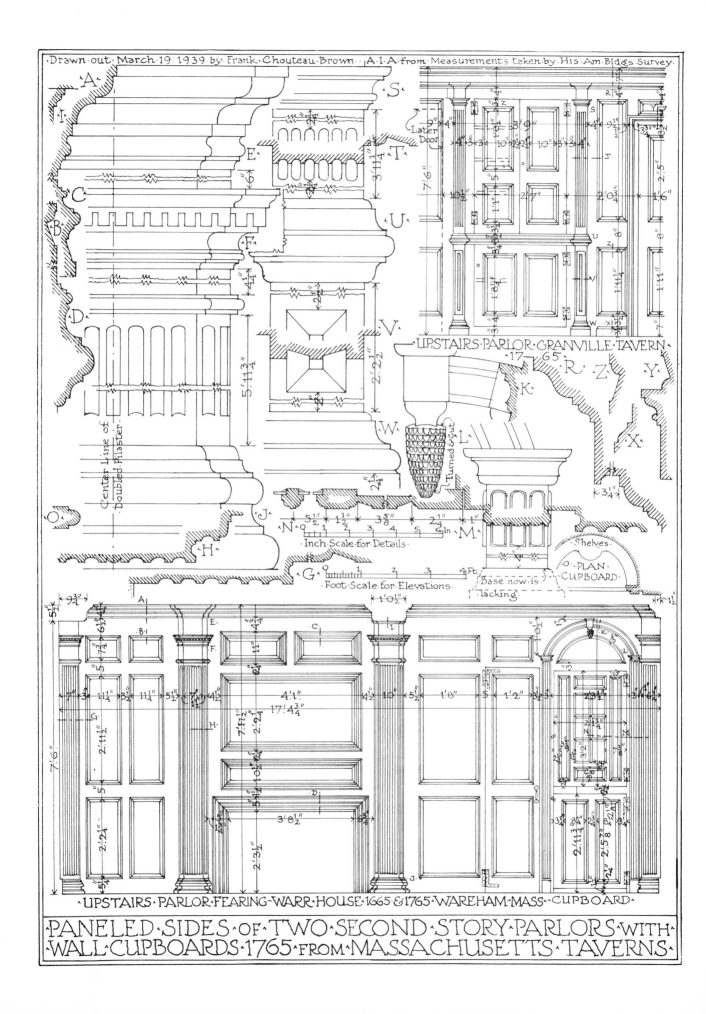

Center Line of Doubled Pilaster.

Later Door

·UPSTAIRS·PARLOR·GRANVILLE·TAVERN·
·17—65·

Inch·Scale·for·Details·

Turned & Cut

·PLAN·
·CUPBOARD·

Shelves

Base now is lacking.

·Foot·Scale·for·Elevations·

·UPSTAIRS·PARLOR·FEARING·WARR·HOUSE·1665·&·1765·WAREHAM·MASS·CUPBOARD·

·PANELED·SIDES·OF·TWO·SECOND·STORY·PARLORS·WITH·
·WALL·CUPBOARDS·1765·FROM·MASSACHUSETTS·TAVERNS·

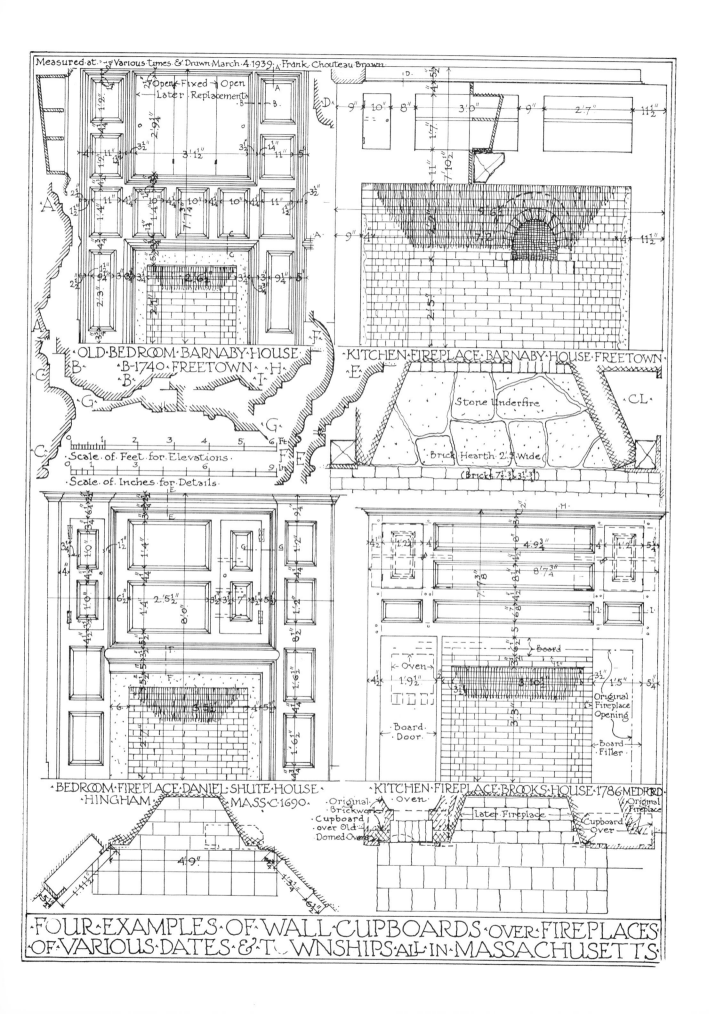

Measured at various times & Drawn March 4 1939 Frank Chouteau Brown

OLD·BEDROOM·BARNABY·HOUSE
B-1740·FREETOWN

KITCHEN·FIREPLACE·BARNABY·HOUSE·FREETOWN

Scale·of·Feet·for·Elevations.
Scale·of·Inches·for·Details.

Stone Underfire

Brick Hearth 2'5" Wide
(Bricks 7½×3½×3½)

BEDROOM·FIREPLACE·DANIEL·SHUTE·HOUSE·
HINGHAM   MASS·C·1690·

KITCHEN·FIREPLACE·BROOKS·HOUSE·1786·MEDFORD

Board

Oven
Board
Door.

Original
Fireplace
Opening

Board
Filler

Oven
Original
Brickwork
Cupboard
over Old
Domed Oven

later Fireplace

Original
Fireplace

Cupboard
Over

·FOUR·EXAMPLES·OF·WALL·CUPBOARDS·OVER·FIREPLACES·
·OF·VARIOUS·DATES·&·TOWNSHIPS·ALL·IN·MASSACHUSETTS·

Fireplace and Cabinets, First Floor Rear Bedroom
DANIEL SHUTE HOUSE—c1690—HINGHAM, MASS.

Fireplace and Wall Cabinet, First Floor Bedroom
BARNABY HOUSE—c1740—FREETOWN, MASSACHUSETTS

Small Wall Cupboard Beside Fireplace
OLD DENNISON HOUSE — c1727 — ANNISQUAM, MASS.

Tall Wall Cupboard in Old Kitchen
HASKELL DWELLING — c1650 — WEST GLOUCESTER, MASS.

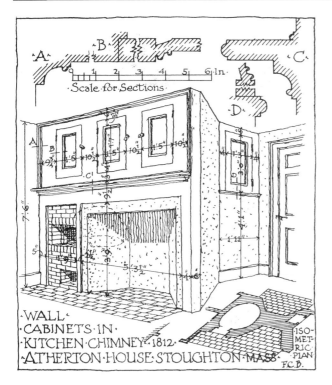

·WALL·
·CABINETS·IN·
·KITCHEN·CHIMNEY· 1812·
·ATHERTON·HOUSE·STOUGHTON·MASS·

ISO-
MET-
RIC·
PLAN
F.C.B.

balanced interior arrangement. And the many simple and ingenuous ways in which the balance of the early colonial or provincial plan is adjusted to the *un*balance of the room wall, is a study in itself; without a comprehension of which subtleties no one can appreciate or follow the ways of the original New England builders.

In the more informal early cottages we find a tendency to locate open shelves or closed cupboards in recesses over or about the most-used fireplaces, either in kitchen or living room. Examples of such "cubbyholes" abound along the seashore, on Cape Ann, or "down on" Cape Cod. They are found about New Bedford, the Narragansett coast, or along the "North Shore" into Maine. They are also common in the inner farming sections, Worcester County, or the Connecticut Valley. A number appear in earlier volumes of this series; such as those dealing with Cape Ann (Vol. III, Chaps. 10, 11, 13, 14, 15), Old Newbury (Vol. VIII, Chap. 11) and the Smithfields (Vol. VI, Chap. 10), and Tiverton, R.I. (Vol. VI, Chap. 5).

In this chapter a variety of examples has been

Old Kitchen Fireplace and Wall Cabinets
JONATHAN BROOKS HOUSE—1786—MEDFORD, MASSACHUSETTS

Fireplace and Wall Cabinet in Paneled End, East Parlor
OLD RED HOUSE — c1745 — GILL, MASSACHUSETTS

Fireplace in Old Kitchen and Standing Cupboard
MAJOR JOHN BRADFORD HOUSE — 1674 — KINGSTON, MASSACHUSETTS

gathered from in or near to Worcester County, (page 212), from western Massachusetts (pages 217, 218, 223); a couple from Rhode Island—near the coast (pages 216, 225), and the balance from Rockport, Nantucket Island, Cape Cod or the inland roads leading toward it, near Hingham, Plymouth, and about Cape Ann. Most of the illustrations belong to the less formal types, placed in and about fireplaces, over mantels or brick ovens, or sometimes partially concealed within the treatment of a paneled wall. One or two verge upon the more formal arched-top design of the typical

Small Hanging Wall Cabinet, Lean-to Entry
WILLIAM HASKELL DWELLING—c1650—
WEST GLOUCESTER, MASSACHUSETTS

open corner cupboard, for the display of gay china or burnished pewter, along with two unusual examples of cupboards contained within the paneling of upstairs inn parlors —of the same date, 1765, but of widely separated geographical location. Although most of the illustrations are of recessed wall cupboards, a few show simple, free-standing pieces, of early pine workmanship (as on pages 216, 223, 224, and 226) of which at least one or more are expressive of the once-prevalent kitchen dresser type, in its earlier and simpler manifestations, now so seldom complete when found.

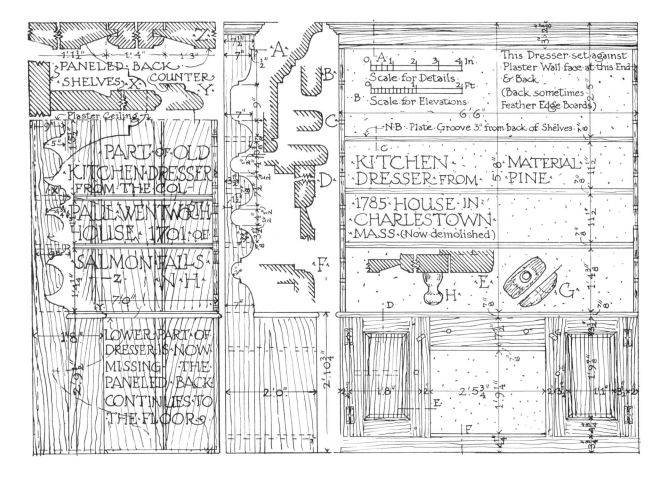

Historic American Buildings Survey

Center South Room Fireplace Wall and Cabinets
OLD TAVERN INN — c1700 — MIDDLEBOROUGH, MASSACHUSETTS

Fireplace and Wall Cabinet in Center Room
AMASA GRAY HOUSE, LITTLE COMPTON, RHODE ISLAND

New Hampshire Pine Wall Dresser

NOW IN DAVID SHAPELY HOUSE—1718—BASS ROCKS, MASS.
(FORMERLY AT KILLINGLY, CONN.)

Wall Dresser in Lean-to

WILLIAM HASKELL DWELLING—c1650—
WEST GLOUCESTER, MASSACHUSETTS

INDEX

References to photographs are printed in italic. Boldface references are to measured drawings. The volume number is indicated by a roman numeral.

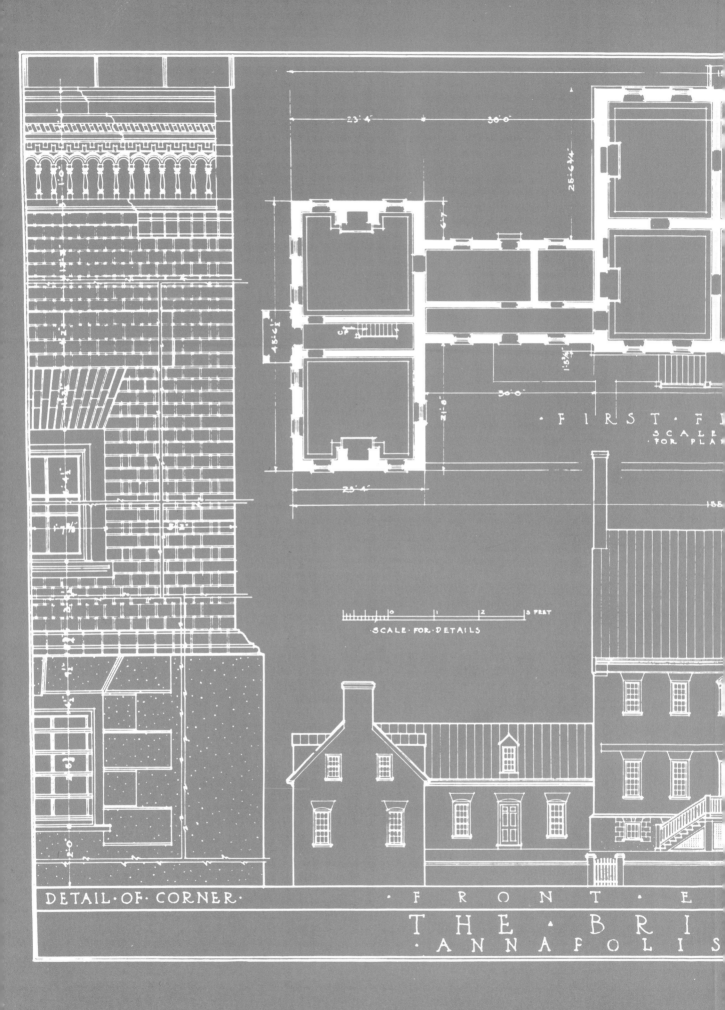

DETAIL·OF·CORNER·   ·F R O N T· E

SCALE·FOR·DETAILS

·F I R S T· F
SCALE
FOR·PLA

T H E · B R I
· A N N A P O L I S